Kentucky Review
2016

Editor-in-Chief
Robert S. King

Associate Editors
Joan Colby, Helen Losse, Mike James,
Ken Craft, Marie Lecrivain, Sara Clancy

Assistant Editor
Rachel L. MacAulay

Design and Production
Diane Kistner

www.kentuckyreview.net

A Good Works Project

ISSN 2376-9920 (print)
ISSN 2376-9939 (online)

Cover artwork, "Snowy Horses" by digicla
Cover and interior book design by Diane Kistner
Georgia text with Insignia titling

Published by Kentucky Review (a division of FutureCycle Press)
Lexington, Kentucky, USA

ISSN 2376-9920
ISBN 978-1-942371-50-2

ABOUT THIS ISSUE

This is our farewell issue of *Kentucky Review,* but we can look back over the past three years and take pride in the work we have published. Nearly 400 poets and writers have appeared in KR, many well known and several who made their literary debuts.

As always, I thank all of the editors of *Kentucky Review* (see the title page) and also Diane Kistner, the Director of FutureCycle Press, who designs and publishes KR. We are proud that KR is one of the press's Good Works projects, with all proceeds from sales benefitting Action Against Hunger.

Of course, I thank all our readers and contributors and trust that everyone will find a lot to like in these pages.

—Robert S. King, Editor-in-Chief

Contents

Contributor Notes

DAVID ADÈS

The Janitor

The janitor likes to fly under the radar.

Better than a drone, he floats
under the invisibility cloak of bucket and broom,

of mop and wet rags,
noticing every speck of dust, missing nothing.

He is the hidden vault, the repository

of every transgression, every furtive glance,
every swept-under-the-carpet secret.

He holds it all in the avid gleam of his eyes,
in the whisperings of his lips

uttered for no one but himself.

He is never asked and does not tell,
immersed in the labyrinth of his library,

an infinity of shadow lives,
sad tales, unhappy endings.

From My Gallery Days, #23

Louisa, wearier than a mime in a straitjacket,
dubbed her self-portrait pointillist, though Z
joked it was connect-the-drool. She couldn't've
cared less about the blogs, nodding to the bank.

I rambled the rooms of the Frederick repeating
only applause & $$$ can balm Louisa's wound!

I don't know what it was about her follow-up—
"the provincial madams"—that wired the devil,
Ed Hauser raging in the dailies & so much vitriol.
In the end, the 9th Circuit had to bang the gavel.

> It's easy to be intimidated by discord,
> I've found that most rebels wanna be liked.

> It's easy to be intimidated by discord,
> I've found that most rebels wanna be liked.

Burying her brushes, a CNA in pressed white,
Louisa hocked her oeuvre to a resident gynecologist.

DIANA ANHALT

I Suppose When Death

elbows its way through your door and presses
her mouth to your ear, she'll jumpstart memories,
send your thoughts pivoting like a sunflower

following light to, perhaps, your first taste of pineapple
or the day you mastered, at last, the dead man's float,
fell in love, scored a goal, bungled one. In one single life

such an excess of possible firsts: The time you wrote
your name in wet concrete, lost your stride, an old friend,
your front tooth. And if, as promised, your life flashes

in front of your eyes, do you get to omit the things you'd chosen
to forget? Those smudged fingerprints of failure and the words
you'd neglected to swallow? Of course, like the moth

that remembers the flame, you may return instead
to the last time, fingers buried deep in damp soil,
you breathed in its scent, planted a magnolia

or opened your mouth to rain, shared the bath with a lover,
finished reading the story you wanted never to end.

If I Have Learned Anything About Love

If I have learned anything about love
it has been from your hors d'oeuvres-platter
approach, your way of serving yourself
in cubed and toothpicked bits
with a breezy little laugh, *oh, this?*
this is all I had in the fridge. No I know,
we didn't meet at that kind of party,
but maybe I wish that we had.
Isn't that the only way to know each other
intimately, seeing the exact shade
we dye ourselves in contrast to the crowd?
You, my sharp turquoise, neon
and body-pocked from so many
paring knives, always make yourself known.
If I have learned anything about love
it wasn't from that boy who was a man
who was a boy, or from the faces
and ceiling tiles hovering above a crib.
Every pulled tendon, splintered
bone you went ahead and walked on
was a lesson. Remember that party?
More organ meat on trays. It takes a toll.
We're not girls people picture like girls,
but we did stay up until dawn
like you're meant to, and ordered pizza
like you're meant to, watched meet-cutes
on that 20-inch screen. That didn't teach me
much either. How terrifying it is to live
as an X-ray, how fearlessly you walk
around that way, your skin like a cobweb.
You'll never make a soldier, so utterly
unarmored. If I have learned anything about
love it's been by noticing your eyes
have a habit of opening incredibly wide—

shocked by my suggestion that you find some
shield to keep your body apart from the air,
from the maddeningly thin air.
Why do you throw yourself so resolutely?
What do I serve of myself?

Still Life With

it always starts with gesso a primed canvas
prepped for each brushstroke each palette knife swipe
it starts with a sketch hand sweeping across canvas enough to mark

the desired path it starts by angling the easel starts by fiddling
with the curtains the light should glint hint at shadows
of soft down on the skin of a peach it starts with a sigh starts

by eyeing the composition asking *is it balanced* switch
the pitcher to the right *there now* it starts when you stop
stealing glances at the apple-cheeked model across

the room it starts with a donned smock poised brush slick palm
she is prone by the portraitists starts by subtracting a grape
that one there pushing it past your lips and biting down

A Prayer to the Artist for Eternal Life

—after David Hockney's A Bigger Splash

The house and pool lie low and level
under a corrugated sky.
Only the electric splash beneath the diving board
jolts the painting's perfect world.

Time will never fade that flat, flawless house
nor thunderheads blot the boundless blue above.
Water will never prune the unseen diver's hands,
or glittering sun freckle and pleat his skin.
Grown children will never come weeping to the house
to plant a For Sale sign in the clipped green grass
and slide a cover over the pool.

Hear me, David Hockney: Melt my flesh into pigment
and prison me in the perfection of painted water.
Suspend me in your spotless, changeless world,
caught forever in an upward arc
as I follow rising bubbles
to the light above.

Paying Bills in August

It's the other side of high summer.
Hostas and clematis petered out, the light
filtered by cloud and leaves still green.

This messy summer has accumulated.
It's time to pay the bills, add up the costs,
get ready for joe-pye weed, goldenrod
and giant zucchini. This wasteful season's
detritus is about to descend, dissembling as beauty—
turning leaves, late flowers, drunken bees, ripe apples—
all that Keats cemented in my eye.
But beauty's just an idea, death real
and the road to it, exhausting.

See the Truth in a Chicken

THE COYOTE, hunched and coiled by the squat coop door, had the biggest chicken, Lisa, already neck-broke, in his teeth, when Johnson finally fumbled his way up and out of sleep and on to the back steps of the house. He was able to get a shot off as the coyote hurtled the fence.

Heat lightning thumped behind clouds. No storm, yet, but hot enough for that. The summer storms can blow up real quick, nasty enough to drop tornadoes out the sky like fingers touching down, stirring up the land like a drink, and then others were gentle, ticking against the windowpanes like someone was there and then wasn't.

He whispered the other scrambling chickens back into the coop, talking to get them settled and fill that hollow behind his eyes, roll away the lump in his throat. It was late. He could go back to bed. He didn't move until a while after the chickens were silent. Behind him in the dark, skeletons of houses rose up along the curving road scratched through where forest once had been, stopped just short of his back fence. The city wanted the house, but the city and their new development could go straight to hell, with its representatives banging on his door to complain of his chickens, that he had too many. They called it the chicken provision. Because they'd stretched their limits, at first to and then beyond his back fence, he was subject to city zoning.

"Reckon they should call it the fuck you provision."

That was one of the last jokes he'd told his wife. A smile cracked her paling face. She'd gestured with a finger, waggled it a little, and he leaned into her tissue paper voice.

"You keep on about those chickens the way you have and the city'll lock you right up," she'd whispered. She was gone a few days later.

She got sicker, he got more chickens. He came to understand them. They'd mill around at his feet as he whirled feed out to them in dusty arcs. They were there. They did not leave. They left the presents of their eggs.

Lisa was there in the morning, head angled all wrong in the dirt by the fence where the coyote had dropped her. Sophie and Bailey shuffled over, pecked at the dirt around his feet. They knew, they could mourn, too. His second shot had perforated one of the gray fence planks about halfway up, and when he went to cover it up with a plywood scrap, he just started banging at it with a hammer until a full-on hole gaped in the planking. He put his face to the hole and saw the fresh piles of lumber, close enough to make out blood stars dotted along the far edge where the coyote had run. A breeze kicked up dust in the smell of rain and heat.

"People say chickens don't have a personality, no soul," he'd told his wife. "People know shit. You look close, look a chicken in the eye, you can see the truth in a chicken. Distinct as folks."

He followed blood dollops to where high-shouldered turkey vultures, old men at a buffet, tugged at the coyote, in a burnt-out ditch by the new road. It was hot and the road shimmered but the breeze began wailing, the bruise of a storm rising over the trees.

It was a Sunday and no one was working at the houses, and on his way back he stepped into one, walked through the rooms and pissed in the center of the room he figured would be the kitchen. He zipped up and walked room to room, whistling, his noise bouncing off the bare plywood and studs. The world outside turned dark in a sudden rush of wind, and he looked out at the chaos, straight across to his house just as a bolt of lightning stabbed fire through his house. The lump rolled into his throat when he thought about the chickens, how close they were to the house.

"You think about the chickens too much," his wife said once when he'd come in worried about a hawk he'd seen. The sickness made her look old and made him feel that way.

"How you going to say goodbye to me if you can't even stop worrying about a chicken a few minutes."

"When that hawk's shadow crossed the yard they all froze, a good ten seconds they stood there, and then scrambled to any shadow they could find. People know shit."

"You know they don't last, either," she said.

"I know it."

He was out on the new paved road that ended at his fence when Myriam, a chunky leghorn, appeared, awkward and frantic above the fence, lifting herself with the clumsy flap of wings, neck stretched, squawking above the thunder rumble and terrible crumpling noise of flames behind her. She landed and plodded several steps, pausing to shake out her wings. And then behind her, the others pushed through a gap in the gray fence, falling over one another, away from the flames and towards Johnson. He called each as she appeared: Bailey, April, May, June, July, Augusta, Weezie, Sazy, Lizzie, Hannah, Anna, Rosanna, and Sophie.

The flames jumped from his house to the weed stalks in his yard and then to the pile of lumber just beyond his property and then to the first of the frame houses. Wouldn't his wife be happy about all that.

SANDY BEACHES

Personality Disordered

BEN MICHAELIS, a clinical psychologist, said in *Vanity Fair* that Donald Trump has "Textbook narcissistic personality disorder." He is not the first psychologist to have diagnosed Trump as having a personality disorder. Not one of these psychologists engaged in a private conversation with Donald Trump. Not one of them is qualified to diagnose him as having a personality disorder.

I first heard the term "personality disorder" from my dad as we were driving home from dinner one night. He was a psychiatrist and therefore knew what he was talking about. Borderline was the phrase he used to describe my 13-year-old friend who required an immense amount of attention. I would later hear this term in regards to my mother, bad drivers, people who didn't tip, and anyone who was disagreeable.

My mother, who also worked in psych, would use this phrase too. Dad had a personality disorder. My teachers had personality disorders. The woman she went out with for lunch who "forgot her wallet" had a personality disorder. They were everywhere.

From a very young age I started to doubt my personality. Was it, like so many others, disordered too? As far as I was concerned, I didn't have a personality. I was quiet. I didn't voice my opinions. And worst of all, I didn't want to stand out. If I had no personality, surely I was disordered as well.

Years later I talked to a therapist about my fear of being labeled as "borderline." He laughed. Although he reassured me I didn't have a personality disorder, how could he tell? If someone could be judged as personality disordered based on the way they drive, who was to say I wouldn't be diagnosed too someday?

My therapist reassured me again, explaining to me what a personality disorder was and why I didn't have one. Instability in relationships. Poor self-esteem. Manipulative behavior. A fear of abandonment. The criteria seemed suspiciously vague. If that was the bulk of a personality disorder, no wonder it seemed like everyone had one.

One year ago a friend of mine was diagnosed as having borderline personality disorder. I visited her in a psychiatric inpatient facility just a few minutes from town after she tried to commit suicide. Heather, who was not close to her family, had become extremely depressed after seeing them for an extended period of time. When I saw her, she was wearing all black and her voice sounded small.

Heather sat on a green floral couch in the living room area of the facility, with dozens of women's magazines scattered around her. How to lose ten pounds. How to decorate to impress. Everything you need to know about carbs. The headlines were daunting. Heather didn't read women's magazines. Immediately I knew something was up.

"They want to send me to a residential treatment center for borderlines," she said. I could tell she had been crying.

"That's ridiculous," I answered honestly. "You don't qualify."

"But that's what people are saying." Her voice was heavy and tired. Her whole body looked fatigued with the weight of depression. All at once I thought of a medical professional, maybe one like my parents, who could have called her this. They must have diagnosed her on a whim. She said the psychiatrist saw her for ten minutes.

One year and a good counselor later, my friend is fine. She did not go to a residential treatment center and instead went to counseling. Her eyes light up when we talk. Her voice is no longer small and distant. The women's magazines are gone.

Recently I went into the same psychiatric inpatient facility as my friend for depression. I couldn't eat. I couldn't sleep. I felt like I was failing miserably at life.

Reluctantly I walked down the long hall to see my assigned therapist, Bill. I was terrified. I had a sinking feeling that he was going to diagnose me as having a personality disorder.

"Why are you crying?" The therapist asked.

"I'm afraid of personality disorders," I said nervously. I then told him about my parents and the way they used the term. Bill took a deep breath and shook his head. I could tell he was different. I could tell he wasn't the kind to diagnose on a whim. I could tell Bill was listening. Bill looked at me and lowered his head, "It sounds like your parents may have a personality disorder."

Bad Acoustics

THEY WEREN'T OFFICIALLY anything now. That said, all the lingering had proven more difficult for Gina than Lars. He smiled bright in soft green shadows, awaiting his introduction. The MC was particularly flaky that evening, continually shirking her duties in favor of casual flirtations and the sting of rising foam in her cup. Gina watched the girl's slender hips sway up the stairs, grinning at the mere thought. Here he was, for your viewing pleasure; another willing contestant.

Lars introduced himself with a waning certainty, brushing long curls behind his ears; a sip of beer, before licking his lips. He'd sat next to her the previous hour, but hadn't said much. The temptation to grab his hand, locking fingers and expressions, had passed in-between comments on the competition. They all weren't as bad as he said. Some just needed practice, either too young or merely disinterested with the faint glimmer of gold medals and pats on the back. There was some Nirvana, Beatles, Green Day, and of course, The Dead; all faint imitations or lackadaisical renditions by comparison.

She almost recognized a few players, some transplanted directly from campus, a week's worth of facial hair ripening from the pores. Their red eyes made her regret previous decisions. Lars usually brought enough weed for two, but they were past obligations. Gina could only sit and listen, the initial feedback of his six-string giving her chills with a twist. She no longer saw the local rock star expecting the world to notice. Producers and agents weren't waiting in the wings. The Broken Screen Door had only atmosphere to offer; the ineptitude of stage fright and stomached butterflies drifting right through him like sunlight past the shades.

He began with a fever, fingerpicking, walking up the neck before sliding back down, crafting arpeggios from thinning air and listless sighs. She didn't recognize the song at first, its melody cracking as if being administered by a school nurse. *Hold up either your left or right hand if you hear the frequency.* Gina's ears popped in the middle, light beads of sweat pirouetting above her forehead. The booze wasn't enough, his voice surrounding her, poking away at each follicle; hairs on her arm rising only to fall again.

The tune passed in thoughts of the prior year, the places he'd taken her only to wander off. There was displacement in their scene, an unfortunate pondering that no one would be around forever. Bands broke up or switched members. A death was mourned with all-night bonfires, turmoil and bug spray rising in clouds under flashy stage displays. Lars was looser in the moonlight, nearly forgetting to zip the tent flap as half-conscious nobleman passed with their milkmaids, slurring the words to a song the writer could only regret.

There she would lie, feeling everything, and wondering if it'd go on forever; a swelling thump in her chest from subwoofers and expectations. He finished to dwindled applause, reaching for the capo and reintroducing himself. She stopped clapping soon after the rest, smiling to save face. Conversations stumbled in and cluttered; a general disregard for the old ways, before screens became Gods, providing their brethren with necessary answers. Gina blamed every voice for talking out of turn, marking their days in inconveniences. She wanted to scold the silly children like a mother. What was it with kids these days? Why was she still young enough to be lumped in with the rest?

Lars barely glanced in her direction, slowing his strum, every syncopated wallop of the strings building to a greater tension. His voice, although crisp, began to dissipate. He was losing his breath, pushing air past dry lips, slurring a parade of words she knew too well. There was a charm to his manner, a raw sexual appeal that made Gina wet when she least expected it, right before the chorus. He howled into the microphone, kicking up a storm of static through the speakers. Some began to cringe and take phone calls outside, a few dough-eyed dropouts, bobbing along, holding their beers and lighters high in support.

Gina considered going to the bathroom, or home all together, calling friends she'd lost touch with or putting on more lipstick. In the end, waiting for him to finish was easiest; an applause greater and yet somehow more distant rising. Saving the axe, Lars barely listened to the next introduction, his body bouncing at every limb. "So they think I'm great, don't they?" he suggested, hand slinking past her shoulder as he sat.

"Yeah, of course," she forced a smile, then shifted to the stage.

He was a stick of a boy, clean-shaven, and peaceful from the first word on. "Hey, I'm Stuart, and I wrote this one." His fingers weren't calloused enough, the reliable crawl of a melody pouring forth in-between chord changes. He sung of those uninterested, a lush display of cattle galloping off towards the slaughterhouse. She dug the metaphor, but missed a few phrases when Lars leaned in and whispered. "So I'm gonna go outside and get baked."

"Okay," Gina nodded.

"Are you coming?"

"Yeah, I'll be right behind you."

"Okay," he smiled like nothing had changed, almost tripping over her back chair leg. She caught a baron whiff of his cologne mixed with sweat. It wasn't new anymore; he'd smell that way for at least another five years. Gina listened till the end, then stood over sloshed acclamation. Passing dissolved egos and indigo slide screens, she paused near the door as Stuart started again. He was angrier now, letting the air catch fire as it exited his throat. Gina considered whether that girl was even present; the one who'd broken Stuart's heart, made him pretend like someone would give a damn. She sighed and stepped out. He wouldn't be winning the prize money that night.

DICK BENTLEY

Poem

YOU HAVEN'T HEARD of me yet, but my name was once linked to a poet named Edward Starling. Starling gave me a brave name, some stanzas, and a few similes.

Starling and I were ambitious. He wanted to be a famous poet, and I wanted to be a famous poem.

We met at a writers' workshop in upstate New York. I was smitten. He was young, tall, and athletic, like a trapeze artist at the circus. He held me for a while as we swung wildly above the crowd. Then he tried to flip me to the next trapeze artist who was an editor at the *Pig Iron Review*. I was rejected. I tumbled through dark space, into a floppy safety net of inconsequential adverbs and mystical observations.

Still, I had another life coming.

Harlan Winslow gave me a title. It was quite minimalist. He called me *Poem*. Were we as a love affair, or just a literary friendship? He scoured his notes, hoping to improve me. He seemed tortured by me. He read me over and over as if I were a prayer. I spoke back to him. I was teaching him how to write, but he gradually got the idea that he was going to starve unless he made money on his art. My best friend at the time was a limerick named *There Was an Old Man with a Nose* who had escaped from one of those children's books. *Old Man with a Nose* was also looking for a new author. We created some stanzas out of exotic symbols we knew—like sun, wave, stars and sand. We placed them in Winslow's mailbox along with some crayons and paper. We anticipated a response. We waited and waited until we forgot about him.

When you are a poem, what you mean to say and when you mean to say it are indistinguishable. It may be time to leave the circus. But even indistinguishable poems possess meanings. We poems drift across the earth, seizing poets even as they walk down the streets past pizza stands and parking meters. We live in art galleries, auditoriums, bookstores, malodorous bars, the gray keys of laptops, blogs. We live in notebooks bent in poets' pockets. Sometimes we can be seen popping pills and laughing over what a poet just wrote, wondering which lines we find insulting and which are pure joy.

I always thought, "Oh, if only I could crawl inside the head of a man and eat his thoughts, then I will begin to live my life."

I met Jerry on a computer dating-service network designed for poems and poets. He became my romantic ideal. He was both beat and beast and he scared me. He was very tall and his eyes were green. We found a small apartment in an old house in Amherst, Massachusetts.

We live there now. I follow him around while he thinks about me and mumbles me. Some days he thinks he has written poorly, but I tell him, "You can always go back. You can learn to change me with a little grace. That's the point. That's love. That's bliss."

The Look on the Face of Scarlett O'Hara

She went to a dance in a makeshift ballgown, tired
of having to bear the full weight of a blue-eyed rage

at Union artillery barrages undigging the fresh graves
of the Confederate dead, a rage fed by the fires of loss.

The end of one world and the beginning of another is in
the look on Scarlett's face. And the fear of starvation, too.

Flirting at barbecues insulated her from the reality of death.
From the battle noise of a new nation creaking into existence.

The squabbles of men are at the heart of her needing to dance,
why she appears about to order Rhett Butler back to perdition

or Charleston. All that death is why Rhett is about to comply
if Scarlett will concede life is short. And a pity to squander.

My mother was born in 1932. Raised in eastern Kentucky.
Loved the Old South. She had read *Gone With the Wind*

as a girl. Saw the movie. Before she died, I bought her
a music box that played "Dixie"—Rhett held Scarlett,

doomed lovers embracing by the staircase as if *Tara*
is the name of where we go when we leave this life.

Prospero, Passing

Death is the tempest I am in the midst of now.
How can I unlock my own chest?
What sprite carries my breath in invisible hands
down into fathomless depths?

What can I control now?

I make my daughter to sleep, who makes me
to die? Somewhere in my books
the answer must lie.

It is the magic of breath, a full force
I believe in. But its tide is leaving me.

I thought my lungs unfathomable,
deep as storm-tossed ocean waves.

Now my breath is as water in my lungs,
a rattle of bones, a spell I cannot undo.

I am drowning in my own breath,
here in my landlocked bed.

The Island, After Prospero

it is the vast silence each day that offends me

each day I forget the feel of a girl's footstep

only the whelks' cold progress fill my days

once there was a spirit once there was a darkness
        each one spinning something like a web over me

now each day something like a thread dissolves somewhere inside of me

now even the barnacles seem loud

the waves always retreating and each day more listless

the wind plucking out its own wings and refusing to sing

once there was a man who talked to me in my own language
        each day teaching me something new about my past

now each day something else leaving me another word and another word

now the empty sky pulling itself tighter and tighter over me

Travel (Dream Poem #9)

Seems I loved his brother in another dream, seems
I smell a sweeter nectar at the lips of strangers
before night becomes a shell, spell
gone cold. As if he climbed over a wall

to take that place, and we are late again
for something and it's in some
deserted country as before, paperwork
to fill out for we travel sharp and undirected

(cast myself again as castaway with stowaways)
(this was civilization of some sort).

Dodgy streets we come from. Sit together, bones
apart but he's so sweet I know how we will sleep
tonight, skin to skin brown to white in a camper
just beyond, or there is straw to lie in if it comes
to that, folded with the sweetness,
strong embrace at flesh.

Turn that last corner and there's your room,
your love. I wonder what you'll think
but then I see he might be you. That they all
might just be you. Spirit lifts his lips.
I wake up diving on and on; it's over
when the walls come up, but never fully gone.

Before the Blood-Moon Eclipse

Yours is not the world's astronomy. Here one body
drawn against another is effaced. Explain your stars
to me: your Mars
your Mercury your stair to Venus
pole-star singular out there
love at once centrifugal and still. I am your moon
or fetal flower bloomed
stripped down to where the core lies hold my body
heavy down against the surface
of the world and let the rest rise up as lace
against my holy tree the milk perfume
this haze of stars would like to signify.

Tonight these clouds may part above the ocean
about to show the blood-moon wonder
shine from silver wall a mirror at the edge
of sea-sky universe
crowd along the beach all our lights extinguished
broken-glass arrangements of refracting stars and bodies
moon to stir us into silence: divination
all these sightings quests to make it weave into a cogent
planetary fable explains what holds us here
apart and wondering

Blood Moon

LET'S BEGIN: A little girl walked home from school. A little boy followed her. When she opened the door to her house, he stepped out from behind a bush and frightened her. But she knew who he was. He lived with that old woman who had a cabin deep in the woods.

Let's backtrack: There was an old woman who lived alone deep in the woods. She never wanted anything to do with men (or women), but she wanted a child. She wanted this child so badly that she cut off all of her hair and buried it with the tail of a donkey and the eye of a bat (She didn't mutilate the animals to acquire these things—she ordered them from Amazon.com with the guarantee that no animals were injured in the acquisition of these items). The spell worked. A little boy was delivered to her door the next day. He was brought by FedEx in a box labeled Handle With Care.

Let's continue: The little girl invited the boy inside her house. Her parents weren't home from work yet. She was curious about the boy. She asked him what it was like living in the woods with the old woman. He said it was lonely, but they played all kinds of games; and he didn't have to go to school, because she taught him everything there was to know about the world. The little girl looked at the wise boy and smiled.

Let's look ahead: The little girl and boy got married by the light of the blood moon. It was a secret union until the girl started to swell with pregnancy. She tried to hide the bump, but her parents soon discovered it and cursed the boy who had done this to her. They dragged the girl to church and begged the priest for his forgiveness (which he denied based on a belief that parents should never leave their children home alone). It was the old woman in the woods who made things right. She cooked up a spell and dissolved the pregnancy. All that came out of the little girl was a little trickle of light that flew up into the sky and became a star.

Let's look at the end: The little girl's parents sent her away to a private school on a small island in the middle of the Mediterranean Sea. When the old woman in the woods died, the boy went wandering around the world in search of the girl; it was the star that led him to the island. And there she was, all grown up and more beautiful than ever. They renewed their vows and then had another child. This child grew up to be a wise sage. He is now 1,000 years old or more and people say that he has the knowledge of immortality; they line up from land to sea, from all parts of the world, to speak to him. But he only nods his head and smiles.

ROSE MARY BOEHM

Prena, Housegirl in Nepal

I wish I could remember.
My mother. I can't see
her face.
My owner beats me
when I spill her perfume.

Sometimes I see things
on that living-picture box
she watches when
I have to bring her the sweets.

We often meet at the market,
Ashmi and I. She said
the king is dead and we'll
be free. Free—for what?

All I know is sweep, wash up, light the fires.
Ashmi said we could get married.
Why? I asked. She laughed
and called me a child.
She behaves like a woman.
I am already 14, I think.
I even have a room of my own.

She won't get married either.
Nobody wanted us when we were small.
Who would have us now?
There was a stream near my house
when I was little. It gurgled.

ACE BOGGESS

"What's the Point of Robbery When Nothing Is Worth Stealing?"

[question asked by Alex Kendall]

A lamp will catch scratch at a yard sale,
too that forgotten paperweight with portrait-
under-glass of a woman's silhouette.
Everything has value to a thief—
needy, adding up pennies to fix himself,
to pay off his debt to the shadows.
My stepbrother learned that last month when
importunate hicks from the hollow where he lives
cleaned him out, stripped his trailer,
took goods plus the urn with his father's ashes.
He said, "I bet they dumped him in a ditch somewhere.
Even if they're caught, I won't get him back."
His eyes tried to swallow back the grief,
cheeks restrained in a crimson straitjacket
as he thought about how a bucket
full of powdered bones might find
the black market, blackest,
someplace a good man wouldn't walk
without at least a razor in his shoe.

She Slips

She slips from the chair, her body
more fragile than I'd expected,
the bones in her fingers unlike mine.
They hold a glass of tea.

I hold a glass of tea, and her fingers
become strange companions—
they could touch my hair
or shield me when I can't sleep.

Their whispering foreignness
moves me, the way they call
the waiter for more tea, a cup
of pudding with walnuts and bananas,

a wave to the ships at Maltepe
where she'd been in love before.
Before I knew the boundaries
of love, and why some women wait

with bruised fingers, broken skin,
ten dollars, joy in the form of a man
wandering Black Arm Street
in search of bread and a place to hide.

Water

Laid off from Union Tool,
he's Muddy Water's brand of *ready*.

No more pitchforks, open fire.
No more paycheck either,
but perhaps even this, a blessing.

Why shouldn't he start over at 50?
Cast his net to the other side?

Mohawk River's lovely this time of year.
Canoe upstream to Lock 18
and it's cedar waxwings, kingfishers—
a pair of bald eagles if you're lucky.

But he doesn't own a boat,
and the trail winds along the canal
where you can't see a damn thing.

Smoke from Route 5S finds its way
into the pocket of his flannel.
Crickets scatter. A lone crappie flops.

He could crack a can of Utica Club
on Casey, where there's always
a fire and a girl who knows

or move wife and sons
to Kentucky—pay is slim,
but cigarettes aren't taxed

like his back and maybe men
don't stoop like they've spent
their lives portaging barges.

Or if he cared about such things,
he could be baptized again.

He knows a few who've done it;
seen Jesus in a barmaid at Reggie's,
hills over the Valley.

As if aspersion, immersion,
even salvation itself could make up
for the shame of sitting in a class

full of college kids who don't know
this town is more than an exit
off the Thruway, trove

where you can mine for diamonds
that aren't really diamonds at all.

His ancestors settled this land;
survived massacres, revolution.
They figured things out.

How come all these years later
he's the indentured servant?

He'll drive up Vickerman,
try to make out his father's cross
through rain that falls like holy water
on vugs of quartz and granite.

Endurance

Based on The Prison of My Youth, *a sculpture by Rick Claraval*

Caged within his father's words—
"You're worthless," "Shut your mouth,"
"You don't know nothin', boy."
"Why are you so stupid, boy?"

Shame bolts pierced everything
that made him. Cylinder of hate
created by his creator:
la parole that imprisons,

a tropic doom chrysalis that
became *la langue,* the system
his preformed body writhed
within, the skin of his dreams,

filleted by sound chisels,
a genetic code of conflict,
never escaped but evolved
into art, a metamorphosis

of triumph—what separates us
from animals and from parents
who act like animals.

CALEB BUSCH

Outer Limit

IT WAS THE SUMMER all my acquaintances suddenly vanished. Not my friends. Not my neighbors. Not my co-workers. Not the people I talk to semi-regularly. Acquaintances. No one interesting. Just people I had met, nodded to, exchanged handshakes with, passed on public transit. Those on the outside. Drifters. Not my mother, for God's sake. Not my fiancé. Not my boss. Not my dog. Not the people secretly behind the scenes, either, the ones we should technically be grateful for. Not firefighters. Not my intern. Not the people running film at the movie theatre. And not the whole city. Just acquaintances. The other people. The outer limit.

Which makes me hesitate.

Because what if everyone on the outer border just disappeared. The not-quite-so-important-but-not-quite-so-unimportant. The people I forgot about. The people I could remember given a picture and telling quote. But only maybe. I can't help but think it's my fault. People don't just disappear. But this is also natural, I think, for people to blame themselves. We all believe we are the most important variable, the shit, the Great Bambino, the Jupiter of the solar system, pulling on everything. But in reality we are nothing but a small moon circling around the cool surface of Pluto, dormant, biding our time. We're tiny. Unimpactful.

Though I can't help but think it's important.

Because when I found out I was sitting in my office, sipping tea, finishing a novel or an obituary or maybe a letter to a friend I hadn't spoken to in a long time, since sophomore year. I just knew, then. Something took me. Maybe spiritual. The bank teller. The barista. The hot dog vendor. I knew they were all gone and nothing would bring them back. The mailman. The hairdresser. The waitress at Outback. And they were just acquaintances. I didn't know her anymore, though rumor has it she was a chiropractor. Who knows. But I asked somewhere in the body of the letter, just to be sure, something like: "According to Pew polls, back disease is a serious problem and currently under-rated. By any chance would you have professional thoughts?" It's corny. She probably forgot about me. It's a good chance she's gone. We used to write letters in high school, though I'm sure it would come as a surprise. I don't know if she's an acquaintance, or maybe slightly more, a half-friend, and if that would violate the rule, the rule of only acquaintances. Because I care somewhat. Or if what *I* think matters.

Because it probably doesn't.

But I'm writing this anyway. Because I'm feeling sad. Lately the world has become a lot more permanent. We grow up knowing, *knowing* that catastrophe exists, that people go. Important people. Brothers, girlfriends, aunts. Uncles, grandparents, cats.

Pharmacists. But no one thinks of the outside. No one thinks about the outer limit. Because who cares? No one wants to think about it. Because why should they? The world is big enough, without making it any bigger. But I'm writing this. It's late. My office is a bit messy and for some reason you're on my mind. It's cold out. I'll finish the letter. And I can't shake from my mind how finite the world is. I can't help but wonder if I'm special, if these disappearances are just happening to me, or maybe, you, anyone, if I'm the only one out there, if to some I am nowhere in sight.

WENDY TAYLOR CARLISLE

Letters from Umbria

Caro, I have come to a land where monasteries spoil the hills
and centuries of saints and acolytes amble over consecrated stones
over the vaults of older gods. Here barrel tile mimics the tile of my rotten
childhood and sparrows scuff the treetops, masquerading as angels.

Caro, the sheep who graze beyond the sagging wire fence are tended
by a dog who guards them against predators like me. That dog
is the white dog of safekeeping not one of the black dogs
I've known. I long to stroke her, to call her silvery teeth to my hand.

Oh, Caro, the cedars, hollyhock, the rubble and rust, the scenic
weathers are my familiars. I should have them with me always.
Heel on stone, stone on stone, thigh on thigh, dog on dog, this home
like the home we come from, has not settled. It has shifted and chafed
and eaten up its trees and sheep and seraphs. Why is it I stay,
Caro? Why do I always reach out my hand to what wounds?

The Possibilities of Crows

If he calms their hunger crows will return
when he will not

notice, bearing gifts. Sea glass, light bulb
shards, pearl

button, silver hinge. When crows stare
they are remembering

what slight might shade his next poor choice,
wrong turn. These are the birds

of "If I only..." wise as to why they are called
a murder of crows.

Still, those offered gifts that shine
leave him to wonder

why these crows will not blame him,
wonder how long

these dark birds will continue to bear
his constant harm.

Have Gun, Will Travel

Terrible business, this world, the sides of barns
charred by endless drought and sun, the bleached
bones of leaning houses in fields of weeds.

Now smallpox enters the plot, the old yarn
raising voices, Pa off to get the vaccine. A reach
to get through this half-hour. There are creeds

we live by, a shiny chess piece where quick
shrugs resolve misfortunes. Our mean,
wild west ends this way, rough but clear: evening

crushed to cinders, horses calmed, gun tricks
a quick out.
         Paladin has the best line: "Think about
what's good in the world,
                 what's clean."

For Stella on the Day of the Dead

There was no funeral, but we hung bronze
Soleri bells in the palo verde tree that shades
your spot. I thought you might prefer that crazy

sculpture of a bird you bought made of hatchets
and springs, but it sits too heavy on its garden
refuge and we leave it fixed to its future.

Instead, we put up a hummingbird feeder
that drips liquid sugar, an offering sweet
as baklava to your final desert home.

We placed a rock shot blue with lapis lazuli
and a sphere of handblown glass. I helped dig
the hole and thought of a poem but never

wrote it down. We offered no prayer to the afternoon
and we did not carve your name. But each time I make
Greek coffee in your small copper pot

I turn over the empty cup as you would have
and read a moment of you in the grounds
like a psalm.

CLAYTON ADAM CLARK

1983

—after Encased—Four Rows, 1983-93 *by Jeff Koons*

In the year of cell phones, Internet, the first
artificial heart (he lived one hundred twelve
more days), and my birth, Koons started to make.

While I yawned forth head first from the vulva
of my parents' married mistakes, Koons conceived
twenty-four basketballs (of two brands and three

different skin tones), in original packaging,
in four columns of six—plus futuristic
plastic building-block casing for each ball—

and called it *Four Rows.* Of such creation
some people say, "Anyone could do that."
In this case it's me: that year suicide bombers

murdered three hundred in Beirut, the IRA
bombed UK Christmas shoppers, four million
starved to death in Ethiopia, and when Koons

was done a decade later, my parents had only
made a basketball team of sons and killed
(like half a million Americans that year) a marriage,

but I was (sure I was) uniquely angry. It takes
so long to see the constant: encased basketballs,
my little travesties. How lovely, though,

the singular surprise to tilt one's gaze
and finally see *Four Rows* as four rows.

Mousing

His dead mother's spring traps, well-seasoned
with peanut butter daubs, failed their task,

so he pushed a new glue trap behind
the oven and left for a night's work.

After, with a fork, he flicked the trap
onto the floor. Smaller than his thumb,

a mouse lay fixed at its side, right legs
pinned under the skull and ribs. Its shit,

the small, abundant releases, stuck
in like fashion. The pretty gal said

at the hardware store, *These work real good,*
though a touch inhumanely. He pinched

the trap between his finger and thumb
and hoped the mouse still lived till it writhed.

Dammit, he yelped, the trap adhering
his index to the tail, and peeled it

away, straight into a plastic bag.
Outside in the dawn, he heard a squeak

but wouldn't look in the bag. A plea:
For a favor I'll tell all you want

to know. He spoke into the plastic,
whispered doubts, then raised it to his ear:

No one can save you. He laid the bag
on the lawn and stomped it with his heel

once, as asked, then twice more to be safe.
The second catch was dead by the time

he got home, the fight fossilized—prints
of clawing, living. A manic heart

bursts as the mind bucks for freedom from
the skull's grip. The third and fourth worked on

breaths and bore no concern for the man
who tossed them into the kitchen trash.

He prayed for grace and hush unmoving
in the house no one would seize him from.

Tumble Brook

The brown trout of Tumble Brook
are gone, the stone wall
and the stump we used to meet
to rest our backs against at noon
after following ripples upstream
under sycamores, gone too.

Gone the caddis flies, the filament
of gravel they wove on rock bottoms,
the muskrat holes in the mud bank
and the owl we woke one afternoon
from breaking branches
off a willow struck by storm.

It's not the freeway killed the brook,
the new homes on the east branch
or even the frack mine pump that
lights the neighbor's well on fire.
We took the road to heart, yoked
it always through years of doubt

that this could last, and we were
sure, like friends reliving
their animal rites, our favorite runs divide.
The heavy fog that hides the ripples
on a fall morning tells it true,
each old step is new. The trail is wide.

At the Farm

The wire corncrib charms her.
A twisted metal cage.
"I'd fill it," she says, "with songbirds."
The farmer frowns, dismayed.
She asks the name of the spotted dog. Spot,
Of course. She says, "it should be
Galahad, gallant fellow like that."
She snaps a photo of the barn.
"Living history." The farmer weighs
Speech on his tongue, decides to stay
Mum. A customer, she's come
For the ducks he'd advertised.
She'd pictured roasted ones,
Flocked with orange sauce and wine
Until his children come
Armed with nets on poles.

Carnival: Midway

Pockets jingling as they swagger
Between the rows of booths where hawkers
Challenge them to try their luck.
These boys need to impress the girls,
Oohing and aahing over tokens,
A necklace or something soft
And cuddly. A throwing arm
Or shooter's eye is what is needed.
And even though they know it's rigged,
They've got to try. Ante up. Lose all you've got.
There'll be no cotton candy or root beer floats,
No Ferris wheel hugging, nothing sweet
And sticky to remember. A guy with sideburns
Says, "Hey fella. That little girl wants to see
Your pitch."

Carnival: Tilt-a-Whirl

To be queasy is how some people
Think of love. Vertigo of desire where
Being swung out of the ordinary
Dictates of balance is enough
To make you think the extraordinary
Will last beyond the mad impulse.
Infatuation, that's the dizzy specter
They said beware of. How what can't last
Can make you stumble as you exit
With the world still out of kilter,
Still spinning in its violent colors,
And look, look, how they line up
Holding their tickets, wanting
The experience of whirling until
The gorge rises in the throat.

The Peacock

"HIS WIFE LIKED THEM," Hans said, "Now there's just the one."

The peacock perched in the loft window. Every so often it emitted a harsh scream. They'd come for the hay. Keri could see it was no good. Old, stalky and musty. God knows how long it had been there, neatly stacked.

The old man, Herman, looked hopeful, wiping his big hands on his overalls. Hans noticed Keri's expression. "It's all right," he assured her. Keri supposed he wanted to help Herman out. The old man, alone since Mag died. Hans was a nice kid; he'd come over as an exchange student and probably overstayed his visa. Keri didn't care to know, any more than she cared to know where Hans was living. He showed up daily to help feed and muck stalls. A reliable kid.

She looked at the hay. "I don't know." Below, in the bowels of the barn, grey ghostly shapes grunted and shoved.

"I could kill you a pig," Herman offered.

Keri shook her head. Still, she wanted to be a good neighbor, a kind one. "I might take twenty bales," she said.

"I could let you have more," said Herman. He kicked at a bale, rousing a fine white powder.

Mold, thought Keri. "Twenty's fine. We've just got the pickup, that's about all we can haul."

The peacock screamed.

Heading home, Keri turned off down a rutted track and braked. "Let's dump those bales," she said. Hans got out and started unloading. "You could keep some."

"Fine. One bale then." Keri was angry with herself. What a charade. Herman's pride had to be salved; he'd never take charity. It might not even be about the money. He could slaughter those pigs. For godsake, he has a peacock! She felt scammed, manipulated. These old guys were country slickers.

"Were you getting a kickback?" she asked Hans. He looked surprised, as if he didn't know what that meant.

"Don't shit me, Hans."

"Herman's lonely," Hans said.

We're all lonely, Keri thought. Everyone who lives alone with no one but animals that demand attention. She backed the truck onto the blacktop; it was getting late, time to feed.

Hans came by in the morning as usual.

"Watch this," Keri said breaking open the saved bale and scattering flakes near the pasture feeder. The bay mare sauntered over, took a deep sniff and proceeded to roll on the powdery hay, pressing it into the dirt.

"That's what she thinks of it," Keri jeered. "You've got a good heart, I guess Hans."

The boy flushed. Keri felt weary. "That old man, he's happy thinking he's pulled a fast one. He probably doesn't have much to feel good about." Hans didn't say anything.

"What about you, kid? What do you feel good about?"

"I like the horses," Hans said simply. "I like it here."

"Even if you arrange to screw me out of a hundred bucks?" Keri raised an eyebrow, then shrugged. She pictured that peacock silhouetted in the gothic window. Hans forked soiled straw into the wheelbarrow. The yearling filly nickered.

Moral dilemmas, thought Keri. Letting an old man think he's still a sharp trader. What was that worth? Maybe nothing. Maybe more than it seemed.

GAYLE COMPTON

Hillbilly Haiku

—for Diane Sawyer

I.

Red rooster
crowing on the bed post—
dawn in Jeremiah

II.

Mauve antique sofa,
deep piled carpet—
Monkey Town dump

III.

Hundred dollar TV,
hair pulling at Walmart—
Black Friday

IV.

Maternity gown,
mortar board—
girl most likely

V.

Apple core
in the ashtray—
got teeth!

VI.

Two herniated discs
from deer stand fall—
Workman's Comp

VII.

White Horse liniment
and Chanel No. 5—
"Do you take this woman..."

VIII.

The snail's silver track in moonlight,
a taste of fresh morning dew—
roundup on Marrowbone

IX.

Cap, gown,
keys to the Dollar Store—
magna cum laude

Hide and Seek

AMY SHIMMIES a soft sweater over her head and smooths it over her hips. She brushes her long brown hair over her shoulders, 100 strokes so it's soft like the warm blue sheets where she sleeps with her husband, Alex. Her husband, Alex, who is also sleeping with someone else.

She hears him moving around the bedroom, humming as he dresses, opening and closing drawers and closets, the normal morning noises that have become so routine and even precious to her. She brushes her teeth as she hears him sing a few notes, which means he is putting on his tie. The locksmith will be here shortly after he's gone. She has finally made the decision, and she won't let herself turn back.

Amy slides a red lipstick over her lips. It clashes with the sweater, but she needs something, anything, to brighten this day she will end her marriage. She surveys her reflection for a moment, and then she sighs. She sinks onto the top of the toilet, reaches for a strip of toilet paper, and scrubs at her lips. The color is almost the same shade she found on Alex's shirts two months ago when he came home from a business trip. She feels a little foolish, discovering his affair in such a clichéd way, and she even made up excuses —maybe it was her own lipstick; maybe she washed a tube with his shirt and it all stuck to his collar. Still, she never has brought herself to ask him, and last week, when her friend Karissa texted her a picture of Alex at a bar with a blonde floozy when he had told her he was working late, Amy had to abandon even that flimsy hope.

She sighs again and tosses the toilet paper aside. The bright color has stained her lips, reflecting how she feels—wiped off, washed out, rejected. It has not always been this way. She reminds herself it will not always be.

Alex rattles the doorknob. "Babe? I gotta go."

"Okay." Her voice sounds natural to her ears. Does he hear a difference?

"I'll see you tonight. Have a good day. Love you!" She listens to his steps fade down the hall and hears the quiet groaning echo of the garage door.

This is the worst part of every day now. Does he really love her, or does he just think he does? Is he lying? Is he just trying to get out to meet that whore?

But now he won't be the only one lying. Alex thinks she's going to the grocery and to volunteer at the soup kitchen downtown. But the doorbell rings, and she lets the locksmith in to begin work while she sits down across from a framed wedding picture, their faces lit with brilliant white smiles, their first dance fading, his hand on the small of her back as she leans toward him in laughter, heedless of the sharp pinch from too-small shoes. Now he has become a stranger, and her very soul is tender to the touch. She should talk to him, but she doesn't know how.

It is like playing hide-and-seek as a kid: cowering beside the basement steps in the dark, terrified she will be seen and found, and terrified she won't.

Morning Train

Outside before the day
breaks with joy, the first sound I hear:
dark whistle of the Ashland train.

It speaks of paths
overgrown, people stepped past,
dreams diagnosed as sleep.

The fading climbs inside me, curls
a last bend, settles soft in memory's slow.

I walk on without it, with it within,
my ribs its worn tracks, my heart its worn rumble.

KEN CRAFT

Parable of the Wren

It's when I'm feeling small,
silenced by the din
of black dogs,

that I consider the wren,
how she bursts from the brush
of stick and contrast, perches brazen

on the deck's railing cap railing regally.
Mere child's fist-fluff, this dowdy
drop of feather and cocked tail

flaunts her joyful gall and outsized song,
deciding where to nest next—the warp
of my dark or the weft of my design.

My Mother Calls

and says I need
to visit my sister
soon

My first thoughts
are selfish ones

No one tells me
anything

because I took my brother's
death so badly as a boy

But I'm a grown man now
in middle-age
only a few years
younger than

the sister who used
to spank me with
a giant metal spoon

or better yet
pretend to so that
I didn't get a real
beating

Mom says
    She's on so much pain
    medication now
    she doesn't always
    know where she's
    at

I feel the ground
under my feet
soaked with lead

I feel the last
aging child
heavy on the heart
of my mother

I make plans
with my wife
and daughters
to visit

and all
the
anger
in
Leadwood, Missouri
wells up
right
here
in the
final
line
of
this
goddamned
poem

The true story
of Leadwood, Missouri is this:

the ground that waits
the blood heavy with lead
the cigarettes we smoked
and beers we drank
the bullets we shot
the bibles we kept
the big company bucks
someone
somewhere
makes.

What the Old Women Do

Stains on our skirts, frayed gray hair,
we take balls of red thread
into the neighborhood to tie up
tulips and mad forsythia. We haven't

completely lost our cars, edging our way
through hilly lots, swatting at bees.
Sometimes we wake up screaming.
Were we running like thieves

all these years, just not knowing
we were dreaming? We see the way earth
and death look alike—tongues touch
top teeth, mouths slacken.

Weeds volunteer, green from the waking
ground. We hear shifting sounds
dead people make. Pine, old whisperer,
sweet in your constancy, we beckon you

out of the darkness. We see in the stars
a sky-spanning hand, gems on its fingers
and wrist, women with talons
instead of feet, faces like our faces,

star born. We eat animals and they
eat us, worms cleaning skeletons.
Vultures pull apart bodies laid out
on a midden, ten thousand clamshells

and human bones. Look over the water
to white wings lifting and falling. Do you
see avocets? Or women street dancing,
striking our feet on concrete?

On the Right Path

In this room written entirely on paper
I find comfort in the nodding and agreeing of flowers; they
tell me that I am not just a crazy woman sitting alone
rambling about dark matter to an invisible audience
sketching out the history of myth in thread and canvas

tumbling inward into myself like a monk
with no god.

My daughter says she's worried about me
being alone all the time, wants to know
what I've been writing but I won't show her.
Someday, I will reveal the secrets
to the future of humanity to her, the origin of snails
the language of pills. But not now.

The Offering

The little bird carries the piece of fruit
from the birch tree to its nest
wriggles its brightly-colored feathers at me
song filling its throat. I carefully cut
another piece of peach, put it on the plate on the deck, wait for its return.

Later, I find that chipmunks have raided
the compost bin, left peach pits
all over the yard. I worry endlessly
about arsenic poisoning, call my husband out to help gather
the little broken bits of rough pit
search helplessly for the deadly hearts

that must be scattered everywhere.
Above, in the trees, the sparrows congregate for the evening
watch me curiously, very much
still alive.

LORI DESANTI

Fossil People

IN THE SPRING, the Atlantic shore is thawing. We walk the snowy path along the water, patches of sand scantily pattern the white expanse. It's these small openings I am looking for; why I come every year at this time to collect things. Before the warm weather coaxes suntanned bodies to search for similar treasures.

With gloved hands, I pick up pink shells and sea glass, throwing away trash that the ocean washes up, when I find it. It is still early in the morning, the sky looks like a warm spread of citrus fruits, the sun with its thick, orange skin waiting to be split open.

My husband points to a fish skeleton with finely patterned bones. I decide it's a herring, snap a photograph and move on. In another patch of sand, a fully formed blue crab rests as if it had been frozen alive. Running from the cold as we all do. The ice fractals creep along its deep blue shell like miniature, white snowflakes.

It's almost beautiful, I say to my husband. I take another photo before placing it back in the sandy grave.

I think I'd like to be buried here, I say.

Right here? he asks.

No, well, in the sound. My ashes. I don't think I want to be buried, not in the dirt anyway. It just seems so final, doesn't it? I say.

He says nothing, but nods. He never liked speaking of death. We're different in that way.

I don't want to turn into this, I nod toward the small snow openings where the earth peeks through.

I don't want to be a fossil, something that can be dug up. Something preserved. At least in the ocean I'll always be moving.

He turns to me, and I think I'm going to be scolded for talking about it.

If that is what you want, he says.

By now the sun has fully risen. It will peel back the blankets of snow. Soon, the heat will scorch the grass and brown our skin. Spring will make us temporarily forget the skeleton trees, the silent birds—and the cold Atlantic Ocean that will rise and swallow everything that was here.

Aesthetic Appreciation

MY FOOTSTEPS, BOOTS on bare concrete, shattering the silence. The grey-clad curator is with that Albanian artist. They're looking at three pictures on the wall. I stop behind them. They don't seem to have heard me and no one moves.

That painting in the middle. I stare, I can't take my eyes off it.

"Hmm," says the curator. I know what she's about to say.

"It's very visual..." She says it slowly, as though the observation is the fruit of elevated aesthetic musings.

Thinking of potential buyers. Maybe one of those collectors she was sneering about the other day. New money and a fondness for figurative work.

"A bird of many feathers." The artist is one of the gallery's best sellers. In his fifties, with glasses and brown hair streaked with grey. Never seems to comb it. Very wise. If he did, he'd look just like anyone else.

I shift my weight from one foot to the other. *Coqueta Crestirrufa,* I remember. *Lophornis Delattrei.* A worn schoolbook. My father pointing, pushing me always to learn. *You'll be the one who makes me proud.* I try to calm my breathing.

"It's colorful," says the curator, stepping back. It sounds like an accusation.

"Yes," says the artist, chuckling. "It had to be. The contrast, you see? Needs to stand out against the machines of destruction. Beautiful and fragile. The one on the left is an oil rig in Nigeria. The other's a chainsaw in a forest in Quebec."

The curator is silent for a long while. The artist falls into a reverie. I cough. Am I supposed to wait here all day?

"Yes," the curator says, "it works. The kitsch—that's why it's good. Is it a real bird or did you invent it? Looks like a hummingbird."

"It's an endangered species. Let me remember the name..."

I clear my throat.

"It's a Coqueta..."

The curator swivels towards me.

"Adela. I forgot all about you." Her glance rests on me for a second. "I was wondering whether you would mind staying late tomorrow? The new show opening, you know...Thank you." She turns back to the artist.

"I don't know what I'd do without Adela." She puts on her caring voice. "She's from Bolivia. Been with us five years."

"Bolivia, that's it! It's called a Dot-Eared Coquette. Coqueta something in Spanish." He closes his eyes. "It has a Latin name that I'd like to use in the catalogue. Sounds more learned. Can't think of it now."

"Dot-eared coquette, hey? Sweet little name. If it's from Bolivia, Adela might know it. Adela?"

I stroll back.

"Adela, that bird there, have you ever seen one, back in Bolivia?"

Exchanging indulgent glances, they wait.

I raise my eyes to the painting, face expressionless. The bird looms, vivid and triumphant in its emerald feathers.

"I never notice birds," I say.

The artist snorts, the curator conceals a smile.

I stand there with my brush and dustpan. "Will that be all?" I ask. "I must clean kitchen."

Burgundy Nights

When you go out Saturday nights
I wait five minutes,
then go over to sit with your wife.

We listen to Sinatra records (kept
in a secret place)
and we slow-dance.

She always shares her burgundy,
her dreams and visions,

how she believes in life beyond death.

We don't love one another
or at least try not to;
our kisses are alcoholic and platonic

And I listen to her many abductions,
her planets made from music and water.

We half-dance goodnight
on the sleek tile of the messy kitchen

And when you get home
she's asleep in bed and I'm taking a hot
bath next door

And sometimes you think you hear
"Strangers in the Night"
as you fumble with your key—

A key that I'll never need.

Enchilada Night

I didn't want my son to be
that kid picking bugs off his T-shirt &
eating them while
sitting in the bleachers with
everybody watching.

But that's who I have—
an obese, alienated bug-eater.
Low IQ but not low enough for the
Special Ed Program.

He's big for ten but they don't want
him on the team.

Robert & I walk back to the car;
he said he wished it was Friday already—
Enchilada Night.

I take his hand & guide him to the
parking lot; his hand is sticky but I don't
want to know why.

We both buckle up. Before I start the car
I tell him that it *is* Friday—
Enchilada Night &
his eyes light-up brighter than any
sphere in the heavens.

I ruffle his hair &
try not to imagine what he has in his mouth.

MARC FRAZIER

Six Notes on Existentialism

> —*after* The Sheltering Sky

1.

The sky hides nothing but ideas of ourselves.
That is why we cry as we fuck below it,
all time spread below, raw.
This intimacy does not connect us.
There is nothing to save me from myself.
As you sicken, I dream a bridge to.

2.

Become my essence: burnt-orange face wrapped:
the blue eyes of an alien among the darker skinned.
This maze of earthen passages leads me to a lair.
I will be kept secure, an exotic creature.
Pages of my heart in words hang as interior decoration.
Naked, he creates me, names my body parts
which I incant as he enters me like.

3.

And: if we had listened to reason
we would not sit with swarms
of flies on buses watching each moment fail us,
nor would I look for a mirror
at every stop to know the actual,
when to travel, adrift, is.

4.

As each hotel becomes less civilized,
we leave our American lives behind
and still don't love enough.
I am more afraid to lose myself than to find myself,
so all is a negotiation between us and.

5.

I am led from atop a young Bedouin's camel,
the carnal my savior—beauty.
The sound of his Arabic is not the sound of my despair.
In time I am left with nothing but this tattered body,
too weak to be the person I want to be.
I cannot go back to anything.
I move on, away from, toward.

6.

When you lie dying in this sand-whipped outpost,
I want you most, spooning broth and medicine that you spit up.
When I step outside to catch my breath, there is nothing.
I gather a few things and move on—to face.

A Hitchhiker's Guide

Gas at Pilot was $3.01, and I laughed,
musing that would get me to the outskirts
of Corbin. But, my stomach snarled,
and I bought a bag of peanuts for a buck.
Four dollars what the wretched require
to breathe another day. I burned my way
and luck out of the mountains, munching
and streaming through the curves of the hills,

tried to ignore the pale sermon of my conscience
as I tailed the red glow of lights past signs
that pointed south, away from invisible voices
that begged for crumbs and the hitchhiker
by the side of the road whose eyes dimmed
knowing I wouldn't dare pick him up.

AMY STRAUSS FRIEDMAN

dusk (n.)—the period of partial darkness between day and night

Inertia,
the kind that mines its
bloodless forklift forward
from wind-song on a puckered
plain, cautions of defenseless
sleep.
A metal monster
whose heart lives   elsewhere.
Or nowhere. Or all over,
like rumor. Like dew,
invisible.
Like the silky hidden thrill of breeze
dusting skirt hems of
children unpatrolled.
Unmoored.
Like the entreaties of beguiling ghosts
from a border
in search of us all.

Last Call

—for Ronda

I'll drive past the farms frozen silent
in these slivers of day, past the silos—
                    the feed's empty flourish,

past thin strips of smoke from old chimneys,
the horses that bare it all,

the fox, gray & red, fur-thick
& the tracks that give them away.

What can I offer? Words fall frozen as tree limbs,
the snow an unrelenting mass.

I'll exit the highway past the empty stadium
find the hospital named Sparrow.

I'll find her—maybe tell her a joke.
We won't talk about crested iris, crocus

coming, or her dog who needs someone
to whistle it home.

Just now

smoke from the chimney across the street
curls its way upward, stops, thins, dissipates.

I'll bring her some stones from the river
she loves. Yes, that's what I'll do.

D. G. GEIS

Ask a tattooist

about true love—

all the Suzannes
smothered under Yin-Yangs

or Michaels devoured
by butterflies;

the Karens lasered off
with no more consideration

than bacon frying in a pan.
Or the Jasons

now stamped VOID,
as superfluous as a bounced check.

Ask a tattooist
about the fickleness of human nature,

the irresolution of erasure,
and the palimpsest of regret.

That the tendency of ink
is to waver enduringly

and the word made flesh
to deliquesce.

How everything reckoned
to a certainty

can so easily
be crossed out;

everything, that is,
except your birthmark.

About which he informs you,
regrettably—

nothing can be done.

A. JOACHIM GLAGE

The Empty Space Where the Future Is

AS A BOY soon to suffer the throes of puberty, young Wendell Blake, after a night of feverish dreams his body understood better than his waking mind, sat up in bed and looked through his window to the slender white oak rooted in the backyard and decided that the tree was, in fact, a female. Not long thereafter, and much to the bemusement of his mother, the boy fell romantically in love with the tree, for which the name *Teresa* occurred to Wendell so swiftly, and seemed to him so natural, that he promptly came to believe the tree had always been called by that name, and that he himself had not assigned it. Such, though, are the ways of young boys: not yet understanding what their bodies want, their imaginations grow strange, even to themselves.

Wendell's mother, as I mentioned, was bemused, but she did not interfere with the romance. The budding sexuality of a boy, she knew, was a fragile thing; even a single humiliating word from her could have proved disastrous. So she chose instead that most judicious of parental options: she would "keep an eye on him." Each day, after he returned home from school, she would watch him through the kitchen window as he sat outside in the yard, settled comfortably next to the tree he called Teresa and whispering to her, sometimes reading aloud or else playing with action figures and holding each one up while explaining its significance.

Wendell's mother did not interfere even when the boy, waving his arms and kicking his feet, appeared to be dancing with the tree. She did not interfere when he would stand motionless with his back up against the trunk and his arms wrapped backwards around it as if he were tied there, or as if, by so fastening himself to it, he were lending the tree his own human face (perhaps, his mother speculated, so that he might see for his beloved Teresa who, after all, had no eyes of her own).

She did not interfere even when Wendell, with an earnestness that is granted exclusively to the sexually innocent, pressed his lips softly against the bark.

It was only when Wendell's mother observed her son drawing faces on the other trees surrounding the yard—multiple times, face after face, one on top of the other, whole columns of them like totem structures—that her concern for the boy began to resemble something more like alarm. To be sure, she admired his artistic ingenuity, the way he crushed and ground the late-blooming blue flowers into a makeshift ink; and indeed some of the faces were even rather cleverly done—he had a flare for random flaws: a crooked nose, a missing tooth—but she was haunted by the thought that these many faces were all just practice, and that Wendell, like some child Frankenstein, was gradually building up to the *final face,* the one he would bring to life upon the bark of Teresa. She feared, should that event transpire, that a dark threshold would be crossed, a point of no return.

*

"So you're sure it's nothing to worry about," Wendell's mother said to Dr. Linda Sayer, the child psychiatrist at the small hospital three towns over. (Wendell's mother didn't want anyone to know she'd taken her boy to a shrink.) She had said it as a statement, not a question, as though she were trying to convince herself of its truth.

"Yes," Dr. Sayer replied. "I find Wendell to be a very happy, healthy, well-adjusted boy."

"But the obsession with the tree...I've read about den-...denda..."

Dr. Sayer laughed. "Dendrophilia? Yes, there are cases of people who develop sexual fetishes for trees. But you have to understand that Wendell is just a boy; children his age develop libidinal attachments to all sorts of objects. A blanket, daddy's raincoat, mommy's lipstick...it doesn't necessarily mean anything. Really it's perfectly normal."

That last word set the mother's mind at ease. It is, after all, what mothers wish to hear about their children more than anything else, more than that they are special or beautiful or talented. A mother's prayers, first and foremost, are for her children to be *normal.*

And so the romance between Wendell and Teresa, having been judged innocent, was permitted to continue. Wendell's mother even stopped watching so worriedly through the kitchen window. It was only by coincidence, then, that on a fine day during the summer of that same year she happened to be looking out to the yard at the very moment that Charles, the family cat, began a slow, clawing climb up the trunk of the tree. Wendell's mother gasped as Wendell flung out his hand and seized the creature and, without changing his expression or even so much as pursing his lips, hurled it down.

*

"It makes him happy," Wendell's mother muttered to herself as she struggled to decide what to do. "He loves that tree." She knew, though, in her heart, which now felt cold, that his happiness shouldn't always matter to her. Sometimes happiness isn't what you pray for. Some happiness you have to snuff out early.

*

Wendell's mother sent the boy off to a two-week sleep-away camp. On the day he returned he found that Teresa, roots and all, was gone. Uprooted and hauled clean away. Wendell's mother stood in the kitchen and wept as she watched her son standing alone in the yard, his miniature suitcase from camp still in his hand, staring into that empty space.

BILL GLOSE

Gloom

It intrudes upon the beginning of chapters
like an unwanted pregnancy, a heralding
that what's to come will veer askew
from best laid plans. The drear of fog,

the pallor of evening, the portent
of a bruised sky—every description
lending malevolence to that hazy realm
of not-quite-dark and not-quite-light,

when shadows dissolve and crisp,
cubist edges shrug into impressionistic
fuzz. But aren't there times when gloom
is welcome, when off-camera becomes

more appealing than the spotlight?
Bliss flourishes on summer days
when clouds can't decide whether
to share their secret with the world,

their gray indecision granting reprieve
to the gardener kneeling in loam,
plucking weeds with gloved hands
and tossing them in a bucket.

And don't forget the first time
a woman invites a guy up after dinner
and chianti, puts on a Marvin Gaye CD,
his honeyed soul spinning them

down the hall to her bedroom.
For an instant, after she flicks
the switch and lamplight bathes
the four-poster bed, her mind returns

to the mirrored image she critiques
every morning, the one she wants
no one else to see. Then she drapes linen
over the shade, and a lovely gloom

enters the room, pulls her into its arms.

Directions to Your Funeral

Take the first road out of town. Any one will do.
Don't stop at your mother's—no time
for that argument, her tut-tutting tongue
and shaking head. Don't pick up friends either.

You can go it alone. You always have.
If a light turns yellow, gun the engine; if it
just turned red, keep going. If anyone honks,
flip them the bird. *Can't they tell you're in a rush?*

Pass by fruit stands; there's no time to feel which
is ripe, which is rotten; no time to feel anything.
Besides, McDonalds has a BOGO special on burgers.
Hold the wheel with your knees as you rip open

a packet and squeeze ketchup onto your fries.
Scarf down both quarter pounders with cheese
until a hot flash burns your chest like a branding iron.
Don't worry, it'll go away; it always does.

Turn on talk radio, the channel with the host
who berates all his callers. Someone is saying,
"I never thought it could happen to me." Laugh
at his stupidity. Then call in to share some clever digs.

When lanes merge, skirt the orange cones and
pinch someone off at the last moment. Roll down
your window and scream at the idiot in the next lane.
Or leave your window up; it doesn't matter. He'll know

what you mean by the snarling O of your mouth,
the stabbing gesticulations, the crimson hue of your face.
Press on the horn. Ride the bumper in front.
Punch the dashboard until your fist is satisfied.

When traffic thins, slalom until life narrows to
a single lane. Ignore the warning signs posted
at the city limits. Floor the accelerator. Hurry up.
Everyone's waiting. And you're almost there.

Our Lady

THE MEXICAN FLAG rippled above the parking lot then slacked as I slid out of the Ford. I walked toward the race track and found a spot along the rail down from the noise and metal of the grandstands. I watched the Ford pass through the exit gate. I checked my watch. A thermometer on a pole with a faded blue Pegasus painted underneath registered one hundred and eleven. I rolled down my sleeves then saw the horse. She lay on the ground. Her muscles bulged. She tried to get up.

"Bad luck," said a young vaquero standing next to the horse.

A gun fired and a pounding filled the air. Horses charged side by side up the straight away, their hooves hammering a trailing dust, the jockeys crouched and whipping.

I turned and saw a stout woman dressed in blue jeans walking toward the lame horse. She tipped her hat against the sun and strands of blonde unfurled against a patch of burnt skin. Now she dropped to her knees and offered words to the animal. The head of the horse lifted then fell again onto the hot desert earth.

About eight of us stood nearby, unassociated, watching the gringa.

"This horse is suffering," she announced in border Spanish. She checked the mare's pulse, felt its forehead, and offered supposition on organ damage and duty. Her mouth moved vigorously but there was no movement in her eyes, only a piercing gaze. Then, perhaps to generate guilt among Catholic hearts, she spoke of Via Dolorosa, the avenue of pain Jesus allegedly walked on his final day.

We stood heavy in her presence, clumsy under the blazing sun.

The gringa eyed us one by one.

"You lowlives are allowing this animal to suffer in the worst conditions," her venture down Dolorosa finished. She leaned over the mare and stroked its neck. "Bring water," she ordered.

Eyes flickered, bodies leaned, pointy boots poked the earth.

One brave vaquero stepped forward and informed the gringa that a priest had been sent for to carry out the last rites. After that, of course, the horse would be shot.

"Shot?" A thick brow quirked under the shadow of her hat.

In the shade of the weigh station, a man in black with the ivory grip of a pistol showing above his belt picked his teeth. A dust devil whirled in the field behind him, lifting trash into the air. The gringa eyed the man, then turned and marched across the white caliche of the parking lot.

A gun exploded. Race horses again galloped down the track spraying the dust of the desert into the air. The rising smut dimmed the sky. A green lizard scurried. Red vested mariachis walked by. Through the white dust above I saw a caracara circling.

I wiped my forehead, checked my watch and looked for the Ford.

The gringa came back with a jug of water. She poured it over the mare rubbing, murmuring in low pitches. Then she looked at us.

"Are you human?" she asked.

She poured more water on the horse. Heat simmered off the black hide.

A man with red-copper skin and a cowboy hat slinked to the horse and felt along its leg. He mumbled something then stood back among us. The gringa smirked.

"How much does the male brain shrink in heat?" She questioned. "Totally? Or do you not have brains only cocks?"

Eyes among our eight blinked, some repeatedly. It felt hotter.

A pick-up with a horse trailer backed up to the mare. The driver opened the door, stood, lifted his hat, mopped his face then scratched his head. He walked to the shade of the grandstands.

"Help me get the horse to the doctor," the gringa commanded.

Eyes darted amongst us. Then one by one we hunkered along the spine of the beast and pushed our hands into the wet muscular flesh. Three hooves kicked with discordant thrusts, hot lies in the Mexican air. The mare snorted. The mass was too much. Her limp leg a dead snake.

"You speak Spanish well," I said kneeling next to the gringa. "Where did you learn?"

She studied me then looked back at the mare.

"I speak Spanish in the present tense," I volunteered. "Can't seem to get beyond it."

"The present is a good place to be," she said in English without looking up.

"You live here?" I asked.

She said nothing, then looked at me. "You're a journalist, aren't you?"

A black SUV drove by, the tinted passenger window filled with a dark mustached face.

"Don't let them find out or you'll be the one shot," she said. "Do you know what this place is?" She nodded toward a low crest in the hills. "See the vultures? They drop the bodies there."

"You know this place well," I said.

"These are my people," she said. "This was my parish."

A priest climbed out of the back seat of the SUV. He stretched then walked toward the horse. He stopped and made the sign of the cross. The gringa looked up.

"Hello, Kathleen," the priest said. "How have you been?"

The gringa looked away.

"I must prepare the horse for the afterlife," the priest announced.

"Then prepare all of Mexico," she said looking toward the SUV. "How much are they paying you?"

"The owner of the horse is a parishioner," the priest said.

"He's a drug dealer."

The priest took a long look at her then kneeled at the head of the horse. We backed away and stood behind our lady as she sifted sand through her hand, the grains washing between her fingers, splashing down against the belly of the horse.

Our Lady rose to her feet, then turned and walked away.

We watched her getting smaller and smaller in the parking lot, the eight of us, collectively pained under the furious sun, as if something good had been taken from us.

Curtis LeMay, His Cigar

He had a joke about the Cohiba,
how it was the only thing
he had in common with Fidel,
how they'd spare the factory
when they came and took the place.

There were times when he would miss it
the way you're supposed to miss a woman:
at altitude with oxygen in the cabin,
on the deer stand,
where it would queer the game.

His subordinates said
you could gauge his mood
—storm or calm—
from the angle at which
it met his jaws.

Fragrant companion from
Berlin to Barksdale,
the Marianas to the Beltway's interior.
At the President's autopsy, some claim,
he appeared wreathed in its smoke.

A steady pull to keep the ember going:
cherry-orange in a stole of ash.
Like Prometheus,
General LeMay
brought the fire with him.

BENJAMIN GOLUBOFF

Home on Leave, Siegfried Sassoon Hallucinates Corpses in Piccadilly

These had all the same impertinence
as the poor sods he'd been seeing in France,
the same unembarrassed way
of offering up, each of them,
his vulgar little secret.

This one, spread-eagle on the pavement by the chemist's,
his face gone black, and the buttons of his tunic
discolored by gas, grinned engagingly
at the stale joke of his own mortality.

Another, in whose countenance
maggots glimmered like Ariel's pearls,
was displayed in the news agent's window.
But this, to Sassoon, was not news.

A legless trunk encumbered
his way to the pillar box.
The legs, each in spattered roll puttees,
leaned casually in the doorway to the stationers.

Sassoon passed by them all briskly
with something like good cheer.
A man of two vocations,
he knew something of the corpses
that the alienist (whom he declined to see)
would never understand.
Sassoon knew the poor bastards were real.

DAVID GROSS

Petroglyphs at Piney Creek

Something pulls us to this place,
where stacks of stratified oolithic
limestone cantilever into rock
shelters in a ravine carved by wind
and water's persistent persuasion.

Twelve hundred years ago
Woodland Indians tapped their
totems into this bluff: earth-signs,
wolves, wavy snakes, mystery dogs,
buffalo skulls, white-tail deer, ducks.

But we always end here,
in front of this elegantly rendered
dragonfly, tinted by creek reflections,
the delicate beads of its body
hovering on wings of riddles.

MADELEINE GROSSMAN

Ice-land

The plane is leaving in an hour
and you think about how
he loves you
just enough
to drive you to the airport
but not enough
to leave with you—

Reykjavik now tastes like horseradish
beneath your tongue and you
wonder
how many lives has
he cracked between his teeth
because he felt like he could
no longer
swallow them?

The Side of the Road

ALL ALONG THE SIDE of the road they stand in single file, faces turned towards the oncoming traffic. In clumps of two or three or larger clusters of a dozen or more, the angle of their motionless waiting is as precise as if aligned to a compass. No head or body protrudes further than its neighbor, giving each still form an equal view of the road. Over countless miles, the figures stand. There are men and women, in no discernible order, interspersed with children holding their mothers' hands.

The relentless sun has not yet emerged. Its early morning rays lightly touch the waiting visages. The knowledge that the sun would ascend in full heat, as it does every day, does not deter the women from their typical habit of dark pants and long-sleeved shirts. They wear no hats. Men sport jeans and corduroy jackets, as if the coming heat would affect them no more with exposed skin than with layers of clothing. Mothers accompany their children dressed in uniforms of navy blue, loosely pleated skirts and white blouses with built in ties. The boys wear pants of the same dark polyester. The children laboriously shoulder school bags stuffed with books and paper. They walk until they stop at unmarked places at the side of the road.

The waiting lines of people carry backpacks on bent shoulders, holding the weight of the day to come in black and sporty bags piped in neon green or soft and sagging pieces of cotton held together with crooked stitches. The bags hold a change of clothes, bread wrapped in cloth and occasionally a piece of fruit. A pair of shoes, cell phone charger and plastic bottle of water might be found. No one wants to go back if they have forgotten something. It takes more than half an hour to reach the road that weaves through the verdant hills.

The road is well paved with cleanly marked lanes of traffic as it makes its way from the center city out to the coastline. Streams of cars pass the waiting people ranged on its dirt shoulders. Armored black behemoths with tinted windows weave seamlessly between rattling tin boxes on four wheels, battered pickup trucks and the buses. Impossible colors adorn the old school buses, turning them from deep yellow into concoctions of bright alternating stripes of teal and magenta or blue streaked with white daisies. On the front, below the driver's perch, stenciled names read, Maria Helena, Rosa or Santa Francisca in looping curlicues.

A mile down the road, a pickup approaches, carrying men and women perched precariously in the open back, their leathered brown faces tucked down into their chests for protection from the wind. A waiting figure begins a slight motion forward but before it achieves full movement, the truck speeds by and the body returns to its resting position among its neighbors in line.

Low hills rise up behind the still figures, hills covered in trodden foot paths and haphazard plywood homes tucked into the leafy overhangs of trees. Steps of concrete, tripping one over the other in their rush to descend, spill onto the gravel shoulder, stopping short of the paved thruway. The road curves around the hills and back again. Straight stretches of highway flank fields of crops where the morning sun chases dust motes in the air. Bare dirt trails crossed with tree roots and stones, worn through with footsteps, make their way down between bushes laden with dust and pollen. The rising sun glitters off corrugated tin huts, poking through the tops of the dark vegetation blanketing the hills. Shadows dapple the endless lines of waiting.

Beneath the constant sound of traffic a woodpecker works away at the bark of a pine tree. Tap. Tap. Tap. A small breeze rustles the grasses threatening to take over the dirt paths. The leaves shift minutely in response to the wind producing a rippling motion above the people listening in stillness. A thrush calls out to a neighboring tree in its nasal voice and receives a slurred *whaaa* in response. The hills teem with the sound of flora and fauna waking up to the day. Only the waiting is silent. No one speaks by the side of the road. The rhythmic passing of cars drowns out the woodpecker's tapping.

Beneath a patch of bare sky, one arm of many arms at the side of the road raises a barely imperceptible amount. The first three fingers stretch straight, the last two curl back into her palm. The arm and hand lower to her side as a bus painted in neon orange over a dark maroon barrels to a stop. Its worn tires screech as the right side of the bus slides on the gravel shoulder, throwing up a cloud of rubble. A man squints. The hand-painted name, above the front grille of the bus, reads, in script, Isidora. Carefully drawn stars in yellow, outlined with thin white paint, circle the name. There is no other writing. From inside the bus dark brown faces peer down at the people waiting, the bright whites of their irises contrasting with the unlit interior. The door opens and the woman moves out of the line. She steps onto the first step and into the bus. The people on the side of the road remain motionless, reduced by one in number.

MIRANDA HANEY

Winter, Buenos Aires

MY MOTHER HAD a different cassette tape for every meal. Bruce Springsteen for chicken pot pie, Abba for corned beef and cabbage, *Phantom of the Opera* for lasagna. She was so consistent with this method, I began to rely solely on my sense of sound to know what was for dinner. I became so dependent on my ears that my eyes had begun to slip away from me. In ninth grade, I got my first pair of glasses.

My lenses allowed me to see faces for all they were worth. My cousin Shelby had freckles. Charlie Geller, the boy that everyone had a crush on, had zits on his forehead. Most importantly, Maria Alvarez had the longest eyelashes I'd ever seen.

Maria played the cello. Though she was only fifteen, she'd received national attention for her talents. She was a first-generation Argentinian-American and spoke both Spanish and English with the most beautiful, precise articulation. During my classes I would ask my teachers to go to the nurse, but instead I would linger around the practice rooms in the music hallway and wait here Maria. In class, she played Tchaikovsky, Vivaldi, and Mozart. But on her own, or when the conductor wasn't paying attention, Maria was partial to the tango.

The first time Maria's music slipped into my ears, I was watching her through a small vent in the wall. At one angle, I could only see her fingers on the neck of her instrument. At another, I could see her face and her eyelashes, gazing into the empty spaces in front of her. She played her songs like hymns, memorizing each fermata, each expression like the word of God. When she finished the song, she packed up all her things. I tried to leave, to avoid being seen as the Peeping Tom that I was, but I was fixed. I wanted to see her hands moving, her fingertips pulling the zipper of her cello case, her slender arms struggling it onto her back. She opened the door and our eyes met. She smiled. I was embarrassed.

"I saw you watching me," she said. "It's nice to have an audience, isn't it?"

For three months, this was our routine. She played, and I watched from the vent in the hallway. She was fine with the arrangement, even happy. After she finished practicing, she and I would talk, usually for no longer than four minutes. Once I invited her to walk with me to her next class. She obliged happily, and we spoke for seven minutes that day. That year we had so many conversations I felt a swelling inside my body grow, cutting off my circulation.

My mother always wanted grandchildren. As an only child, the responsibility fell solely on me and my fertile womb. Until I met Maria, my entire life revolved around my ability to have them. I was going to meet a nice husband and we were going to have two beautiful boys, one named after him and one named after my father, but when Maria

94

said my name the first time, something inside me finally fell into a groove. I was in the right place, a place in which I felt comfortable and prepared, a copper string tuned to the exact pitch it was intended.

I needed to be close to Maria. I wanted her to be there when I fell asleep, the smell of her vanilla perfume in my bedroom in the morning. I craved her opinion on everything, her laugh as the punchline to all my jokes. We never touched. We only embraced in my daydreams, when I reminisced about the tango she'd played early in the day and I saw us dancing, just us in an underground tango club in Buenos Aires.

The air was damp. Her fingers moved gently up and down the neck, somehow finding the exact note she was searching for. We were in the room and we were dancing, but her hands were glued to her cello. Her body was with me. Her eyes fell onto my lips, fresh rosin on a new bow. When the she pressed the lowest string, the sound was heavy and full. My chest became rounder, every sound except the tango blurring into a soft buzz. She lifted her bow, a signal that the song was over. The imaginary audience applauded wildly and we curtsied. I watched her skin bronze in the glow of the spotlights. She picked up her cello and glided behind the safety of the grand curtain and I was alone in the middle of the floor when the lights went off for the night.

I told my mother I was in love with Maria. My mother laughed and said that love is a blanket term for care and concern. My mother was in love with me, she was in love with living in New York City, and she was in love with chicken pot pie. I said I wanted my children to be half me and half Maria. My mother said I would change my mind one day.

I listened to her play the tango 107 times before she graduated high school. Sometimes we would sit out on the balcony of my mother's apartment, Maria playing the cello and I sipping my sweet tea. One time, my mother left the sliding door open when she was making dinner. After she left that night, my mother told me she finally understood. As a parting gift, Maria recorded herself playing *Libertango* on a cassette tape. Maria became the soundtrack to shrimp scampi, and shrimp scampi became my favorite meal.

She met her husband in the cafeteria during our senior year. He was from Chicago, a pianist. His music complimented her in every way necessary, and I wondered if he played her body with the same delicacy. We eventually lost touch and I learned how to play the piano, touching the keys when I can't remember enough.

Contract

SIGN THE CONTRACT. Your baby is born. She is red and wet and screaming and the doctor hands her to your wife and not you. You had come up from your wife's ear to receive the baby but the doctor brought it to the mother, instantly knowing where she belonged. Now the two of you huddle together cheek to cheek as though you are viewing a tiny television set. Squeezing in to see those first few moments, movements.

The forebears, heretofore referred to as "the parents" shall agree to the following.

The doctor says in her own maternal voice, "I'll give you two a few minutes." She brings the tempest out with her. The baby is silent and exhausted, bobbing now on the tide of her mother's breathing. As though borne on the sea.

Shall agree that the child may at any time and any moment utter words that will break the parents' hearts.

Wife is drenched. Tell her you're proud of her and to look at your beautiful baby daughter, just look. Kiss wife on the temple as she closes her eyes and lets go tears that should have been sweated out already.

The child shall be excused for its a priori *ignorance and the parents shall take it upon themselves to secure for it an education, both civil and academic.*

She called you with contractions at 10 a.m. and you immediately took off from work. The workday was over after an hour. You hadn't had a day like this since college when you took the 8 a.m. on Tuesday/Thursday so you could have early weekends. You wanted those early weekends so you could go out with the girl you were seeing at the time. You were dating another girl then, how could that be? How was it that the two of you, now the three of you, were ever not a fixture, an everlastingness?

The couple shall agree that the child is not 100% within their control and manipulation; that the child has free will.

The two of you had met two years after college, online and for the first two months constructed a story of how you met involving you flirting with her at the grocery store. It was vague, because you were bad at flirting and way too good at complimenting. After two months hardly anyone really cares how you met. So you started telling the truth.

The parent(s) shall agree that Life is indifferent to any love transacted between child and parent(s), and this love shall not protect the child from unfortunate instances be they sickness, bullying, bad luck, test inaptitude, failing to make the starting lineup in volleyball...

That was five years ago. Not as long as it sounds, and certainly it should feel longer. Your age changes your perception. Love and age do nothing but speed up the past.

...nor a lone gunman with mental health issues and cold, bored stares as muzzle flashes fill the room like a camera capturing everyone in a candid moment.

Your own father said that having a child was like seeing your heart walk outside your body. Mother is still breathing, and you, father, want to be as close to their heat as possible. Squeeze in a little more. You now begin to miss the vice with which your wife squeezed your hands. All you can do is kiss her and speak in a higher octave.

Finally the parent(s) shall agree that it is their complicit wish and wholehearted desire that the child be alive and well to attend their respective funerals.

Congratulations. It's a girl. You are parents. Was it everything you wished for? Sign the contract. She looks at you now, directly at you. Nameless eyes you barely register as your own underneath folded fat and scarlet skin. Hardly even human. Could you love her any more? Sign the contract. Could you love her any less?

On the Auschwitz-Birkenau Rail Tracks

I wonder how they can leave roses—
these mourners—
as if one beautiful
mass-produced thing
can atone for a war's worth of suffering.
As if it's appropriate to leave a flower to wither and die
in this place
of all places.
I could strangle those roses with hair.
Bury them beneath eyeglasses.
Spear them on gold teeth.
I won't say I could burn them, though that's what we all are thinking.
I want to pick up every flower
and pluck the tender petals,
rip through the bloodless white veins,
let the weak thorns press into my palms.
These things are made to be torn apart,
scattered on the harrowed earth,
and forgotten.
I have lost nothing   myself
but a vial of perfume,
the tiniest Russian doll,
and a ballet slipper's ribbon.
But here I stand, judging, as if I were God,
the tender oblations soft hands have placed here.

For Lilith

They say she chases women and their bloody births
and her shadow rises above cribs
when once crying babies stop breathing.
If you ask, she will tell you:
Before the first silvery light
rose over the cold planes of a new planet
her womb was closed
and though she glories
in taking her lover's member
between her thighs
her own vine grows outward
in delicate tendrils,
forever casting out her lover's seed
in homage to First Man, first love
banished from the Garden.
She will never wear your chaste veils
or stand before a hot kettle
and when she meets Our Lord
it will be in an open field.
He will pluck flowers from her hair
and look upon her moon white body
and wonder that this was the wife
Adam could not hold.
These were the generous hips
that would never yield.
Let her fingers find your most private places
as your bed fills with her feathers, never yours,
dampened with flights never taken
before she tosses her head
and hair black as crows' wings
spills in your face.
Her whisper is an open cavern
at the edge of the sea.

If you turn your head
and only the moon glances back,
a mere flicker of an eyelash,
remember, it was you who chose
to let go of her hand.
She never promised to follow.

John Wayne

Loved Tolkien and hated horses. How many would bet the reverse? As much an invention as any cowboy or soldier he played. He believed in midnight, bourbon and tomorrow. Walked slow and talked slow across plains and desert. He gave up being Marion to become John Wayne. His second name, two single syllables, said quick, like a bullet, or stretched out like a yell in a valley.

David Carradine

Death is a rumor that keeps getting verified. There's nothing profound about saying the truth. If I walk backwards and say my lines I probably won't say them as well as if I walk forward. It's less natural to go in reverse. That's OK. Death's out in front of us. It's that roadblock we can't walk around.

The Windmill

I no longer take myself downtown
and lie on a doctor's sofa.
Instead, I've come to enjoy the few minutes
I lie on my *own* sofa,
books piled high beside me,
a friendly little spider dangling from the ceiling,
its cobweb catching the light.
Little is asked of me
during these moments of quietude and peace
and I am free to meditate
on the red pleated lampshade made of tufted silk
glowing at the foot of the stairs.
Through my wife's lifelong affair
with lamps, I've come to know
all sorts of lampshades—
candelabra shades, coolie shades,
drums, empire, bell—
and to take delight in the sculpted finials
atop the lamps in our house,
finials that are like little poems
made of metal, stone, crystal, and wood.
For Christmas, my sister gave us a lampshade,
a barrel lampshade with golden polka dots.
The crazy lampshade is now the crowning glory
of the iron floor lamp that towers over
and guards my sofa reveries.
The warm light shines through the polka dots
onto an antique leather screen
handed down to me many years ago by my mother.
Painted on the leather screen is a Dutch landscape
with a dreamlike old village by a peaceful river.
In Holland I walk by the water.
I say whatever's on my mind
beneath an old windmill and its cross of golden sails.

The Used Bookstore

It seems like a million years ago
when I worked at the used bookstore
in Los Angeles. Back then
there were bookstores everywhere
and every bookstore had its own personality.
The bookstore across the street from mine
was a literary bookstore that sold
little mimeographed magazines.
When you read the poems, the blue ink
would rub off the page and stain your hands.
I loved that, and also that the poetry books
were specially displayed on old wooden shelves
by the front door, right next to the cash register
so you couldn't miss them. The bookstore
where I worked was known for medical books,
primarily psychiatric books and manuals,
hardbound tomes of profound erudition,
often out of print and hard to find,
like Virginia Woolf's Bloomsbury editions
of Sigmund Freud's monographs.
The front door had a bell that would wake me from my reveries.
I'd look up from my book. Sunlight would spill into the shop,
scattering the shadows and making the dust sparkle
like a billion tiny stars, drifting, weightless in the air.
Sometimes a crazy person would rush in off the street,
looking over their shoulder to see if they'd been followed,
and breathless ask all sorts of mad questions.
To these men and women the bookstore was a place of refuge,
a kind of sanctuary or sacred spring,
but I was almost as lost and lonely as they were
and had no answer to life's riddles.
I was only twenty-two
and didn't know what to say or how to answer
when their words were like wisps from extinguished flames.

But sometimes someone came who just wanted a book
He'd been unable to find.
From behind the counter I would say yes,
I can help you, and their eyes would brighten,
as if I had given them hope
or promised an explanation to the mystery
of why things are the way things are.
I knew exactly where in the store the title was shelved
and I'd lead buyers through a labyrinth of tall bookcases
and place the book into their hands like a prize,
like a palm leaf of victory or triumph.
The readers who sought those rare books
and the street people with their mad questions
are all ghosts now,
ghosts who haunt my dreams
or drift like smoke through old memories
of long hours spent alone in the dim and musky store,
reading Karl Marx or Sophocles,
while outside on the sunbaked boulevards
the jacaranda trees lifted pale blue flowers to the sky.

The Globe

Among spectral gray figures, I stood
waiting on the train platform. I said
hello to the pregnant girl, who looked
up shyly from the globe of her belly
cradled in her hands like a mystery.
Seated on the train I said hello to the
conductor, who checked his pocket
watch and punched my ticket. At dawn
I disembarked in another country. I
hoisted my rucksack and walked the
strange town's labyrinth. I said hello
to the grocer in his long apron and the
street sweeper leaning on his broom.
In the old square's stone fountain, I
washed my face in the cold water,
and turned to face the stately hospital.
I crossed the street and climbed the
wide steps. In the vestibule I said hello
to a Mary statue, who welcomed me.
As I lay in a white gown on a rolling stretcher, I said hello to the orderly.
In a white room, a light swung down,
intense and blinding. I said hello to
the masked surgeon leaning close,
and with the last of my strength lifted
a heavy hand and waved hello to the
nameless anesthesiologist calibrating
her machine, turning dials, so I might
descend to the nethermost regions of
the earth, and greet the lost ones there.

Milk and Honey

Finally I just decided to go,
to follow the wind wherever
the wind wished to take me.
I drove to a forest of pines.
In a tent by a clear stream
I couldn't have been happier,
but happiness was not the plan,
the wind was the plan.
Higher up the mountain
the road came to an end,
so I left the car by the cliff
and walked on, climbing.
But that high up, the wind
was furor and tumult, blowing
and whipping in every direction.
I took off my backpack
and rested against a large rock
overlooking open country,
endless sky, and a red sun
setting over a distant river
ablaze in the dying light.
Then the wind died down
and everything became still.
From the mountaintop, I saw
I'd not cross to the other side.
I was like Moses in his final hours,
looking down on the land of milk and honey.

Kindness

I learned kindness from a near-blind farmer,
who found his best shoes knotted together
behind the back bedroom dresser, then me
with a pair of safety scissors, hidden
among quilts and sheets. Voice never rising,
he sat on the mattress edge palming the lump
that was my head, before saying, "I suppose
it was past time to buy new strings."

Under covers, with air hot and sparse,
the pressure from his ninety year old
fingertips—leathered by years of pulling
fence line—this is what I imagine
grace must feel like.

Clubhouse

MY CLUBHOUSE IS a shrine to the man flipping burgers down in the yard. He probably didn't know when he built it that he was building his own memorial.

Some people are like that. They don't even mean to leave fingerprints all over you, but it happens anyway and you never get those little bits of yourself back.

It's ten years old now, balanced in a stout tree in the backyard where I can see glimpses of the road through the branches. One of the sides used to be open so I could use it as a porch, but I closed it in. Now there's an old braided rug on the floor and a plastic card table against one wall, with a camping cot tucked under it.

If I ever need to, I could live up here.

On the table is a copy of *Peter Pan,* and on the floor is a copy of *The Picture of Dorian Gray.* Brennan, my six-year-old neighbor, has tacked crayon pictures up all over the walls, and in one corner is a robot costume we made him from some old cardboard boxes.

Before too long, I think the clubhouse will be his and not mine. I will have moved out without looking back and he will learn to use this place as something other than a secret shrine. A dinosaur lookout, maybe.

The dog tags hang from a nail on the side of the window frame. I asked for them the first time he left, because that's the romantic sort of thing people do in the movies. I don't want them anymore, but there are some things I can't give back because my dad doesn't know he's dead yet. I still don't know how to break the news to him.

Knives hang on the wall from my summer student trips away. Poland, Prague, Africa, Jerusalem...souvenirs of every time I couldn't make myself stay home and do what had to be done. There's a shoebox full of other things I got overseas, but I hang up the knives. It's nice having them right in the open, things that look exactly how I feel.

Ornate, threatening, but useless.

I wonder if seventeen is the age when it begins. When you find you are able to forgive, or you have imagined everything that has happened before, or that the man flipping burgers is in fact dead and the shrine is no longer as morbid as they might say.

I wondered the same thing about twelve, and about fifteen, but nothing has changed. The facts have not gone for plastic surgery, or changed their name, or moved away. The facts are all the same.

Nothing is the same except what I need most to change.

He wears the uniform like it weighs nothing, and leaves for a year like it's just a few nights. He's forgotten about the dog tags I asked for because he hasn't been in the clubhouse since he built it ten years ago. When he and Mom wake up every morning, their bed looks the same way it did the night before. They fluff their pillows and then turn on the coffee machine without saying a single word.

Every day, the smooth sheets cause a few more wrinkles in me. The knives teach me how to look dangerous while concealing the false, unsharpened soul he has given me.

I don't even know who to blame anymore. I've been through it all. It always comes full-circle back to him.

I blamed him so much, for so many things, that he got worn out. Like the stuffed lamb that is now faded as thin as a cloud. There's nothing left to him. He's dead to me.

I sit every day in the middle of a shrine to a man I couldn't forgive.

I sit, and I wait, and I breathe. Peter Pan keeps me company. The false knives on the wall protect me. The dog tags remind me why I am here.

I am waiting for eighteen. I wonder if eighteen will be different.

Black Guitar

A shadow box attached
to the cracked wall by a steel
string displays a small scene:
a man holds a scythe, walking
in his field as the sun recedes.

Once, in your step-father's
tiny apartment I stared while
you plucked a loping waltz
from an Epiphone, the sound
receding like a blindfold

covering my face. My eyes
drawn to just below your waist,
the crack on the wall damp
from the afternoon downpour, the slow
waltz rings my ears now.

A picture with my arm around
you in August 2002, shortly
after my release, how I wanted
to walk out into a field, close

to where I lived in rural Ohio,
with an easel strapped to my back,
a straw hat on my head.
I wanted to paint you sitting
in that tiny apartment, trace

the crack running down the wall
with a black line, damp, your eyes
almost closed while you strum the black
Epiphone in time, the man alone in the field
with his scythe waiting for the sun to set.

ROBERT LEE KENDRICK

Scientific Wild Ass Guess

I should have been in the dirt by now.
At least that's what the cardiologist said
before he buried a rabbit-shaped lump
of metal under my skin, that won't come out
until it or my heart finally quits.

A fox sprints from tree cover to asphalt,
100 feet across the creek bridge. One oncoming
truck at 51 feet per second. Factor in fog
& indeterminate instincts. 20% that these clouds
will become electric today. .0006 that a tree will smoke
from a bolt. Still, I've found four this summer.

I've put 10 grand on electrode, chip, & wire
to give natural selection the slip. I'm promised
the odds are decent to good,
something like thunder & first drops of rain.

Enigmatic World of the Peccary

Today another clipping, proof he's still out there,
harvesting folk-local pamphlets, whatever's weird
or arch-bizarre from small-town weeklies,
the Times online: outrages of government, race,
gays, his margined scoffs about the gross myopia
and rank absurdities of our doomed republic.

He gifts me Christmas hardbacks I don't have time for,
histories of snails, arcane crime, non-fictions flirting
with fact, oversized mailer from some far-flung town
he's pilgrimed to, van crammed with used-book booty.

Lots of time for roaming and reading after his wife
died in that crash twenty years ago. Today's clipping:
a woman obsessed with peccaries, virtually blind beasts,
neither pig nor boar, who mate year-round and clack teeth
loudly when in danger but make ours ache as we eat them.

Or so say the Mataco hunters who range the Pilcomayo
headwaters that straddle Argentina's Bolivian border.
Reeking of rotten Roquefort, the meat is less coveted
than the soft, durable hides, hence gloves
for wartime pilots, race car drivers, wealthy women.

So the gloves kill men and cover their widows' fingers!
Hilarious! he'd scrawled at the end, no doubt sanding
his hands together as he turned all snout and bristle.

JENNIFER LAGIER

Touring Eden

Broken cypress bisect a coastal ranch,
rolling fields of pink and white callas.
We bump down a dirt road,
across sand dunes
covered in beach grass, sapphire lupine.

A red-tail hawk screams,
spirals above wet lilies,
his nervous talons
clawing, unclenching.

Our bus squeezes through tight gates,
passes barbed wire fencing.
From soft leather seats,
we watch hard brown women,
faces wrapped in bandanas.

They wade through pale blooms,
snap nonconforming flower heads
from purple and magenta rogues
to prevent their reseeding.

I see culled bunches
of curled petals fading,
think of your eyes during love,
feel myself growing
dangerously gaudy with passion.

In the Time of Dreams

Keeping track matters more than usual in a time of dreams,
making lists of what comes back and what doesn't like
day and night. The passages in the mind and what to find
in them. The way what we know comes to us, in waves and drifts.
I go over it as I walk under the sliver of moon above my head
in the early morning walking with the dog over the sand and the dirt
on the backfield. The full day light rises up like in the dream
shifting from one world to another. Parallel universes in the
same place. The blackbirds fly out of the sycamores and land
on top of the palm trees into a quiet world with little wind. In
the dream I am trying to fix a lost relationship, in it I am
willing to ride a bike into the mountains to please my
partner in order to see a lake. I am willing to make concessions.
Plant seeds. Another try at holding all the roots in. But she has
already left, planned a new life, left me in a lurch. Even as I
see the lake in my mind, bluer than even I imagined, and I
clearly see the way ahead as simpler. Easier to map. Past the trumpet
flowers with the little yellow horns, the pink poppies gone
wild, the mesquite full of winter pods. We have walked
up a small hill at first and then down again, over the sand,
past the barrel cactus and the desert grass, long and sinewy.
The path is clear after this. The trail home is easy on the eyes
and the body. Why choose another? Soon, time for a day's work
after a good breakfast. Maybe cut a few pale rosebuds for the
kitchen table. I know they will bloom. They always do.

CHARLENE LANGFUR

It Was Exactly Like Waking Up from a Dream

I thought the poem could be a map to the light
today. Outside, wrens in the bushes. Another
wild line or two, the troubling stuff that comes
because it does and the rest, luminous. After that,
what follows must be love. Or I want it to be.
With all that comes with it, a drift of daffodils nearby.
And a single plan made to go for the good even though
no plan is so bold it holds off all the ill-will, the coldness
of human hostility, keeps all the outer limits at bay,
places of ghost and dragons, and only later, there are
palm trees, lush, with fruit so edible you can eat the dates
right off the ground if you want. Yes, ghosts and palm
trees. And there are keys for the map too, and on some
days there are guides for hire to find what is lost.
How else to get on? Waking up in the light and
realizing what came before, half of it still in the mind.
A second world strangely parallel, with so many memories
And all the rest. In the end, violets in the windowsill,
the dog on the couch upside down with her paws in the air,
a new plan, waking from a dream, right where I left off,
all of it lit up all around and I am following the plan out,
ready for another go.

Painting by Alson S. Clark

Orderly world of cottages and golden hour
Sunlight, a world safe for women and children
In the second decade of a new century,
A world I vaguely remember.
I play my guitar after supper: the chords, my fingers,
The bounce of starlight, the dew, the circulation
of water, confusion. Clark painted
Capistrano, the blues of the pure sky, the kinship
Of the sun in stone, of 1919, of a handmade guitar
Reverberating in rooms of plaster and shadow.

RUSTIN LARSON

Just as Fireflies

Would light the spiky chambers
Of the grasses,
So we children
With our little bones
Would illuminate our hands
By cupping them
Over flashlights
And marvel
At the sunset hue
Of our blood and flesh
And mark
How dark
Our skeletons were,
Their black outlines
Shining under the surface.

Bachelor Party

—for Luke and Kent

We climbed the rocks at Lake Vesuvius
and saw a man enter into the shallows
from a cliff peak.

And as the splash bounced up,
taking with it breath and sadness,
we agreed the kids of Scioto County
tell great stories.

That night, we ate steak on tinfoil
and blood puddled black in the moonlight.
We considered how sandstone

had cut our knees and backs open.
How we had scaled the rock face
while wedged into cracks.
How we had knuckled trees by their roots
to pull ourselves over the ledge.

The next morning, we woke to wild turkeys
in the trees above our tent.

ALEX MacCONOCHIE

The Mixing Bowl

She gave me what I'd wanted for a while.
White plastic lid and smooth, clean metal shine
Nothing sticks to long, large enough to make
A cake or batch of waffles in. A mixing bowl.

Colander-nested, solidly light—not the final step
But where things meet and mingle, are emptied
From or left to settle in together, then exchange
Flavors—a salad, say—becoming something new

Through sharing. Small gong that chimes when rinsed
And knocked against the tap. Shadow-mirror
Tilted over dishes, wide mouth now almost half
A flattened sphere. Self-contained yet open-ended gift.

ELIZABETH McMUNN-TETANGCO

Lost Ski

My father lost a ski
as a young man. He hit
a tree. I picture
this as a small painting:

the white
woods, and the cracked
ski; my father thrown
onto his side, panting
with cold.

I never asked him
what the clouds were like that day,

or how he felt,
weaving too
fast while his heart
guttered, a small
wing,
in the thick forest.

If I could, now I would
empty all his pockets;

I would read the bent receipts
and save the coins.
I would keep

all the lost things
somewhere more

safe.

The Woodbine's Song

What is the telephone pole good for if not the woodbine?
—Ruth Stone

If you were that vine growing
where party lines used to vein
the countryside,

          and neighbor
listened to neighbor, you'd climb
toward the untouchable

human sounds humming
into the wires' sway.

          Hugging
its tarred and deadened skin, you'd

hunger for the pole's dull poetry,
the invisible fruit of its lines—

the knit-one-purl-two cup
of everyday sugar and salt—

and the ghost who calls you
through its cords of sound.

ANDERSON O'BRIEN

Slugs

I rise to an alarm at two in the morning
to check my garden for slugs. Beastly things.

They suckle when I am slipper-footed and sleepy,
unguarded in the attack. I hunt them

with hot fingers, pull them from the underside
of feathered leaves, troll them

in damp, humid corners. Artemis in the dark,
I have the moon, a flashlight, and a box of salt.

Hôtel Vanité

The old hotel had never seen herself but knew she was beautiful. She overheard many people in the street marvel at her facade. Some were so taken by her rose marble columns that they paused to take photographs. Her guests included politicians and movie stars. But gradually the compliments grew less frequent and less glowing. The movie stars and politicians were replaced by salesmen and railroad porters. But the old hotel still knew she was beautiful. It was only when the salesmen and porters were replaced by prostitutes and addicts that she became uncertain. One day, after a heavy autumn rain, the storm drains clogged with leaves and the street before her filled with water. The old hotel looked down and for the first time saw her reflection. Many of her windows were broken or boarded, and her rose marble columns were dulled with soot and grime. She began to sob, and as she did, the great terra cotta masks that adorned her balconies began crashing into the street, each with the sound of an explosion. People scattered screaming. Her few occupied rooms were quickly evacuated, and the next day she was wrapped in police tape. A week later a man from the Board of Inspections arrived and taped a notice of demolition to her doors. There's a drugstore on that spot now. It never sleeps and has an atrocious singing voice.

CHARLES O'HAY

Museum of a Lifetime

A man named Walter Cross walks into a museum called The Museum of Walter Cross and finds himself in his own kitchen. The details are exquisite, down to the remains of last night's frozen dinner. In the next room his high school prom is already in progress. "The Air That I Breathe" by The Hollies blares from unseen speakers as teenage shadows sway among the lights. Across the hall, radios, lamps, rotary phones, turntables, combs, oven mitts, and clocks suspended by wires from the ceiling twirl gently. Before him on the floor, every tooth he'd ever had extracted is affixed to a pair of brown wingtips, giving the impression of two small feral hogs. In the Hall of Missed Opportunities, a tropical garden lies encased in ice. And in what is labeled The Party Room, wax automatons of his parents sing "Happy Birthday" to a 20-pound sack of walnuts. "No!" shouts the man, "It's Walter! Wal-TER!"

The Dinner Conversation

THEY SAT ACROSS from each other, their eyes locked on their menus. Above them, the head of a bull punctured the wall. A Patsy Cline song twanged.

"You having steak again, Howard?"

"Looks like a sure bet. How 'bout you, Flo?"

The waitress walked over. Sneakers. Blond. Young enough to be their daughter. She got down to business fast. "Ready to order?"

"The rib eye," said Flo, "can you make it medium? I mean really medium. Not bloody. I hate meat that's bloody."

The waitress cracked her gum. "We aim to please, ma'am."

"On second thought, cook it to medium, then leave it on the grill for a minute or two longer. Not too long. Too long and it tastes like cardboard. Just one more minute."

The waitress squinted, then took her pen and scratched behind her ear.

"Then give me the loaded baked potato. Sour cream only. Don't bother with the butter or the chives. And hold the bacon and the yellow cheese, too."

"So you wanted a baked potato with sour cream only," said the waitress.

"That's what I said." Flo lowered her menu and spoke even louder, like she was speaking to the deaf or someone whose command of English was not as proficient as her own. "A loaded baked potato."

The waitress rolled her eyes and pivoted on her sneakers. Then she faced the old man.

Knowing his wife was difficult, Howard prided himself on being short and to the point. "I'll take the rib eye medium rare," said Howard, "as well as the loaded baked potato."

The waitress raised her eyebrows.

"Whatever it comes with," said Howard, "will do just fine."

His wife, he realized, was in a mood. Her mouth was sucked in like a pants pocket. Her eyes were black beads. There was nothing Howard hated more than her moods.

"So," she said, "what do you think?"

For thirty years, Howard and Flo had played pinochle with their friends Al and Marg. Every Thursday night for thirty years. Then a year ago, Marg had been diagnosed with cancer. Six months later she died. Now suddenly Al wanted to play pinochle again. Could he bring a friend, he asked? He was dating, he told them. He called her *his friend*.

Flo peeled the plastic off the table with her fingernail. She held a shoulder to her chin while she spoke. Coy. Bashful. It was a gesture she must have picked up from a movie. A Scarlett O'Hara kind of gesture.

"If I died," she asked her husband, "would you remarry?"

Howard knew the question was as loaded as his baked potato. He glanced up at the bull before he spoke. "Well, after a certain amount of time, I suppose it's only natural..."

He watched his wife shift in her seat. Howard had tiptoed into a minefield. Now he was sidestepping his way through. "Maybe, years and years later."

Flo's face reddened. "You think it's gonna happen soon, don't you? You think it's gonna happen soon, is that what you're hoping?" Her jaws were locked, her fingers splayed in front of her.

"This is a ridiculous conversation, Flo. You're as healthy as a horse."

"Okay," said Flo. "Let's say I don't die. Let's say we were both single, maybe widowed, and met each other on the street. Would you still be attracted to me? Would you want to date me? Would you want to marry me again?"

Howard remembered their first date. It was 1969. Flo's hair reached down to her waist. She was forty pounds lighter. She smoked grass like a chimney and liked to do it high.

"You're out of sorts, Flo. It's your medication talking. Maybe the new one for your blood pressure. Did you forget to take your Xanax like the doctor said?"

In Howard's mind, he never aged. He worshipped at the shrine of perpetual youth and looked down on those who didn't. He wore a band around his wrist that counted the steps he walked and spandex underwear to help with the chafing. He and Flo had raised three children. Opened businesses and closed them. But when he glanced in the mirror, a college freshman stared back. A full head of hair. A Nehru jacket. A chest as flat as an ironing board. And it never ceased to baffle him why a woman who looked like his grandmother was sitting across from him in a cracked leather booth.

Flo was sobbing. Her nose was red, her lips trembling. She fished some tissues out of her enormous purse.

"I want to renew our vows, Howard. If you really loved me, you'd renew our vows. People have a ceremony. They invite their family and their friends. They even register for gifts."

When the steaks came, they ate in silence and carved the gray fat. The restaurant prided itself on its prime cuts, meats with coils of marbling. By the time they were done carving, what had filled a plate became a fist. Fifteen minutes later, they were full. It had been a long day. They were tired. Even too tired for dessert.

The waitress circled her way back. She looked first at Flo then at Howard. Flipping the pages in her pad, she cracked her gum once more. "Should that be one check tonight or two?"

Neither of them answered. The light overhead swung gently. The bull seemed to grin. And there they sat like bookends, leaning in yet somehow apart.

Caligula's Horse

Although Richard's feet were small like a ballerina's,
his bulk made his Harley look like a roller skate.
Richard would have smiled to learn Caligula rode
his stallion into the Roman Forum, decreeing
it a Senator, as Richard lumbering through gears
up a mountain pass laughed at gravity's failure.
He danced a trucker's jig and sang more tunes
than jukeboxes in both Dakotas, hauling
lacy panties to lift hearts in Pennsylvania
and hammers to beat out fenders in Tennessee.
He straddled wreckage strewn by the careless
taking their eyes from the road to see fields
of wheat dancing in an August wind.
With worn boots he stomped a rattler's head
flatter than a gambler's hidden ace of spades
and downed a slug of bourbon fast as lightning.
Richard's word was a sure bet. Truckers fat
and slender between Bangor and Elmira claimed
Richard for a friend. No torque pounds
could measure their devotion. Had he heard
soldiers nicknamed the child Caligula meaning
Little Boots before he became a sadistic emperor
Richard would not have blinked, knowing the dark
direction roads can take. Richard's pride was not
John Henry's hammer trying to beat an engine.
Richard loved Peterbilts rumbling across the plane.
Bikers and truckers miss his voice as he stepped up
to the bar ordering rounds for everyone, kissing
the pretty ladies. But one's excessive generosity
took him down a road of no return. Drivers approaching
loading docks from Anchorage to Pensacola still look
into their mirrors, wishing they could see Richard's
running lights pulling up from behind.

Down

Meredith, my older sister's friend, affixed
My hands to her hips, my eyes on her
Lips, my flapping feet to the slow jam
Beat on my sister's bedroom transistor.

Her blue eyeliner told me this is how
Two people meet, letting the tune leak
Across their touch, all going fluid, harmonized,
A world in a drifting sea.

And at my first dance, when I caught Jenny,
She said I moved too much, like a fish,
And should get cool and tight and tough,
A bastion she could tap tap alongside.

And from then it's been like catching water
To hold onto a girl.

Laying In

With the first swings you register only the heft
Of maul and the jolt that clangs
From knuckles to elbow
Like scalding water through cold pipes.

You draw on the muscle memory of raw-boned
Ancestors, whose words are written as scars
Crisscrossing the chopping stump
In a language of their own.

"Laying in," my father called it,
And his words come back with each split
Log that tumbles—divided—each to a side,
And with every row the stack gains.

As a kid it was a chore to split wood
Every weekend late summer and fall.
My father could work all day and speak only rarely.
I loafed and wondered why life demanded such devotions.

I have no son of my own, so I speak to him
While chopping wood with his old maul.
I don't need him to answer.
The words themselves summon his attention,

At least the part of him that might understand
The grief that drives this labor,
That most days I find relief no other way
Than by this laying in.

I wonder if this is a form of prayer
And whether all my words to him aren't small prayers
That work like honing stones
For the dull and broken edges of my life.

CATHY PORTER

Every Sky We Invent

The scent of emptiness—
it pours from the hills we walk,
settles at the feet of desertion;
this is where I see you.

Fire alerts us to change—
ashes scatter into piles set aside
for days the wind cuts glass.
Evenings fall into patterns; truth
becomes a warning. Will every sky
we invent be enough to guide us
back home?

It was a gray morning—
as if the sun knew its place.
When the moon slides away,
I sneak inside to find you.

Civics

It is not so much what I am saying,
But the fact that I am telling this to you.

There have been scores of yellow birds
In the field stubble, crows in
The thermals, and this year
Robins are as scarce as new pennies.

Mrs. Habersham, dead these last thirty years,
Still delights in the peonies,
And expects this corner will remain just this way
For as long as God has chin whiskers
And public works is underfunded.

The boys crossing the street are hard
To the edges of their hair. Never mind
They are going for ice cream
And have been waiting all day to do so.
You should not make assumptions
About children so young, particularly
When they travel in packs.

The traffic light
Is still under warranty.

That eight-year-old Ford
Is burning too much oil:
I would have someone look at the rings.

The eldest Donaldson boy will graduate high school
After all. That the sun
Will suck up his shadow is taken for granted.

Visiting like this is what we do.
We even call it "visiting."

There is a story about that bench there,
How it had arms once and a slick
Green paint job and there was an order
To those who sat on the bench.

And then you showed up.

ANA PRUNDARU

Little Adventures

UNDER MY UMBRELLA, my son and I remove spider webs from my grandfather's headstone. I wonder whether it is too soon to call it a Christmas tradition.

"Mom, where do we go after we die?" he asks, as he takes my hand on the way out. Caught off guard, I reply that we go to heaven and regret the stale words as soon as I mouth them. My son nods, but his eyes betray him. The generic answer is as unsatisfactory for him as it is for me.

We pace the path down to a Mom and Pop store for candy, but my son, who usually sports a smile from ear to ear when surrounded by sugary treats, stares through the confectionary display. On the drive to my parents' house, he absentmindedly fumbles with the radio and uncharacteristically neglects to open the bag of candy on his lap.

"You know, your great-grandfather used to say, we create a place made of little adventures and that's where we go," I say and notice his eyes widening.

"What is it like there?" he asks.

"Well, I can only share what he said." I say, relieved to see his cheeks reddening.

"So tell me!" he urges and his fingers find their way inside the candy bag.

I attempt to recall my grandfather's exact words. Instead, I see the place he spoke them; a poorly maintained park near the senior home. I had convinced myself that my company was a welcome distraction from the desolate environment, but looking back, it was him that cheered me up during a period marked by unemployment and a broken relationship.

"Remember how excited you were on your first day of school, when you met your classmates and teacher for the first time and received a glossy paper-bag full of brand-new books?" I say, trying to jog my own memory.

"I suppose?" he says, his chocolate-stained mouth gaping open.

"Great-grandfather said that during our lifetime, we collect endless, bright impressions of people and our surroundings, like smells, colors, or melodies. When they mingle, they become little adventures. We create a special place for them that holds enough magic to become our home later on," I say.

Indeed, on one of our walks, my grandfather stressed the importance of cultivating memories, albeit in conjunction with warning me about detrimental effects of smart phones on my brain. My natural instinct to contradict him for the sake of arguing was only suppressed by the sight of an old man, who stood between the shrubs, stiff-bodied, neck bowed down, resembling a cane.

Curiosity overtook us and we came close—so close we could hear the man breathe—and noticed his eyes were shut and his hands touching the leaves of a jasmine plant, thumbs brushing against its mould-like surface. Grandfather shrugged and continued his social criticism.

The following week, I visited grandfather again and sure enough, we found him in the same spot, his arthritic body glued to the plant. This time, grandfather put his palm on the man's shoulder. Was he OK?, he asked. It turned out the man used to come to the park with his late wife and when she died, he planted a jasmine tree, yellow and bright, just like her.

"So, each time I remember great-grandfather, I can visit him?" my son asks.

"Yes, something like that," I say, thinking, *if only I could.*

Dowsing

To counter the coming pain, I conjure amusement.
Watching them search the blue tracery in my arms,
I note their cockiness deflate to clotting concern.
                Then the arm switch,
the rubber ball squished into my hand,
the unnecessary pumping instructions,
                the tourniquet tightened,
                the brusque thumping of veins.
I plump up hope of a sure aim.

     I always warn them. "My veins are difficult."
     They smile smugly, the bustling nurses
     and technicians in their routine siphoning of blood
     through needles and lines into lab tubes.
     "We've seen a few of those."
     Their confidence smells like diesel.
     "I usually need someone really experienced."
     Umbrage flares. "We're all really experienced."

First try. The needle skewers, nicks, or ruptures the vein.
No response, as their wagging swagger droops.
They clamp cotton and tape over the swelling hematoma.
Second try. The needle enters and sniffs around under the skin,
moving with little jerks, bloodhound's snout in a rabbit hole.
Pain. The nice ones apologize.
     The hunt is aborted. More cotton and tape.
At this point I'm insistent, louder,
about the need for the "most experienced,"
the one "good at this" since that one is obviously
not in the room. Often they try once more, and then
confer in the corner, dispirited vampires in white.

It's never predictable—who the blood whisperer
might be, but upon his (or her) arrival,
                the air in the room changes.
                The barometric pressure goes sunny.

The humbled others dissipate like storm clouds.
With few words, she begins, leaning close,
                        listening perhaps for the flow,
                        touching the faint trill.
Her needle hesitates above the skin like a divining rod.
The tell-tale quiver.
She plunges, and the thin line flows,
so red, so vital, so beautifully obliging.

Dissonance

She never knew I was there,
my twelve-year-old self, peering
through the kitchen window
out to the porch-turned-sun room,
watching my mother.
     There in housedress and apron
she sat on the footstool near the old hi-fi,
     transfixed by Clair de Lune—
each piano note rising from the spinning vinyl
like an iridescent bubble into the long-leaf pines.

The comfortable voices: Perry Como, Peggy Lee,
Tennessee Ernie Ford—our house
         breathed these with ease,
but here was daring Debussy,
     stilling my mother
in the middle of her housework,
rare as a resting bee in the spring orchard.

The memory is evergreen—fresh to this day
each time I hear the piece—
for at that moment,
my mother became   someone I'd never met,
transplanted city girl dreaming something
I couldn't imagine, staring at the tall pines,
their needles flashing brilliance
as they scratched the Alabama sky.

Brace

I WONDERED WHY no one wanted to take the patient to Bayonne, NJ. We'd be crossing three states. The overtime would be ridiculous. You can't make money as an EMT unless you do overtime. Once you put in your forty hours, then you start making money you can survive on. Otherwise you live in poverty where it feels like you're breathing mud.

As soon as I saw him, I knew something was wrong. The nurse said, "See his nails?" I turned his hand over. "Feces."

"You didn't clean him?"

"He keeps doing it." She disappeared into the guts of the hospice. Those places must have hidden rotating fireplaces, walls where the staff dissolves when you need them for signatures, bed change assistance, anything.

We took the patient on the gurney. He wanted to walk, but we can't have patients walk. Even if they're healthy. Even if they're just hypochondriacs. Walking is dangerous. Humans hurt themselves doing anything. This week we transferred a patient who swallowed ten batteries, another who "fell off a mailbox," another who "accidentally" sat on a light bulb while naked, another who cut her nose off with gardening shears, another who lost his foot in a lawn mower accident with an inoperable lawn mower. People are magic at pain. They create injury out of nothing. You can put a person in a barren room and somehow they'll find a way to blood.

My partner drove. I was in back with the patient.

"You all right?" he said. His face had kissed a thousand pitchforks. He had the shame and anger you see on old people's faces sometimes, ones who failed at life. He was in his thirties, but his medical age was mid-fifties. Constant drinking, drugs, fights, and failures do that; it changes a face. It carves reptilian lines in skin.

I wasn't all right. I told him so. I explained motion sickness. I told him I was sick with movement. I explained it's caused by irritation to the labyrinth, a portion of the ear triggering nausea.

"Amazing," he said.

I wondered if it was a pun, if he was playing with the word "labyrinth." I once transferred a "homicidal ideation" patient who did mind games on me to the point my hands shook. She insinuated she'd done endless amounts of stalking in her life and made continual hints she might do it to me. I saw her in windows for weeks. No one knows how to get into a mind like psych patients.

I went to do blood pressure. He told me his arms were too cut up, too. I asked what he meant.

"You know, cut up."

"From?"

"Me."

Scratch marks were up and down the arms.

"What's that from?"

He opened his mouth and took out a paper clip. It'd been between his gums the entire time.

"Can I throw that away?" I asked.

He handed it to me.

"You have more?"

"I forget what I have," he said.

I told him I could do a b.p. on his leg.

"Go ahead," he said.

I rolled up his pants and saw a thick ankle bracelet.

"What's that?"

"It protects me."

"From?"

He shrugged.

I saw my partner watching in the rearview. The freeway was oiled with rain. Rain keeps hospitals rich. Medicine owes its lungs to bad weather.

They say if there's an ambulance crash, the person most likely to die is the medic in back. The patient is strapped in. The driver too. The medic gets thrown into violence.

My partner motioned for me. I leaned up, my head near the spare oxygen tank, a thing shaped like a bomb; my EMT instructor said it could act like a missile if overheated.

No one gets hurt more than medics. Injury creates injury. Car wrecks create car wrecks. Violence infects.

I think about my gun at home, asleep.

My partner says, loud, over the radio, engine, and wind, "He's a sex offender." She responds before I can ask, "It's in his paperwork."

"What he do?"

"Don't ask."

"Why didn't you tell me?"

A motorcyclist weaved between two semis. The sun looked fat in the sky, waiting to blind everyone driving west. I wondered if the sun had diabetes.

The road seemed coffin-colored. The French have a term for when it's sunny and raining at the same time. I forget the French. In English, it's something like, "The devil's beating his wife and marrying his daughter."

I say this to my partner. She drives. The patient watches and my partner tells me the Southern Poverty Law Center has a map of the hate groups in the U.S. New Jersey is so covered by hate groups you can't even see the state.

I go back to the patient. He takes his shirt off.

"It's hot."

It's not hot. I turn on the air conditioner, louder. An uncomfortable cold. Everything suddenly feels so present tense.

"Are you gonna take my blood pressure?" he says.

"I don't have to, if you refuse," I say.

"You want me to refuse?"

His fingers seem darker now. We have three states to go.

"Do you believe in God?" I say.

He seems shocked by the question.

I take his blood pressure.

He replies in a language I don't understand. I wonder if it's a language he's making up. I wonder if he's possessed. Three states. I will watch to make sure he doesn't kill me. I'll take his blood pressure twenty-three times. It will always be low. He's always twelve breaths per minute. The sun sets. It blinds us. We talk into the night, about gambling, his love, his language sometimes sounding like the devil speaking. He tells me about his life but not the bracelet.

On the ride back, my partner and I rarely speak. It's like we want to bathe in silence. She silently calculates how much money we've made on this trip. I think about Nietzsche, Dante's fourth circle of Hell, the possibility of the dawn never arriving.

Live Free or Croak

A SANCTUARY for moonshiners, marijuana growers, and merry pranksters, Frogtown's a tiny community in the piney woods of west central Arkansas.

There's one saloon in town and it's sundown when Hawkins Rogers bursts through its ancient swinging doors.

It has been a long day and Hawk is thirsty.

The joint has a pool table, a jukebox, a dozen bar stools, and five red vinyl booths. The shuffleboard table has been removed to allow more space for dancing and fighting.

It's so dark inside that at first Hawkins doesn't recognize Ruby Canada sitting on a bar stool next to him.

Ruby is a bit of a recluse. Hawk can't remember the last time he's seen her in town. "Ruby, I'll be darned, where've you been?" Hawk says.

"Staying as far away from trouble like you as I can," Ruby half-smiles.

Everyone knows Ruby in the Frogtown area. But only a few know her well. Of these Hawk knows her best.

They had gone to bed together a few years back. It hadn't meant anything to either of them. Both just thought it a friendly gesture on the other's part.

From that night and from other less intimate times being around her, Hawk has learned: Ruby is squeaky clean in some ways and dirty as bus depots in others. She takes milk to market on a horse-drawn cart with car tires for wheels. Soda pop has discolored her teeth but hasn't spoiled her smile. Her eyes are the color of the sky on one of those days in her childhood when she didn't get her way. Sometimes a crow flies over one of those days and she pauses to enjoy its wings.

At least this is how Hawk saw her several year ago. He jotted down these lines about her in a journal he was keeping then. He's thinking about that now when Ruby says, "Let's move to a booth. I have a dirty little secret and I'm dying to share it."

Hawk stands and picks up his glass and her glass and they relocate.

"I terminated it."

"Terminated what?"

"Our baby. We made a baby that night, Hawkins."

Hawk can't tell whether Ruby is playing with him or not.

"This isn't funny, Ruby."

"I agree."

"You don't appear to be too upset about it."

"It was ten years ago, Hawk."

"And you're just now telling me? Why now?"

"I just think you have the right to know."

"Damn straight I do."

"Anyway, now that I'm dying, what does it matter?"

"You're dying?"

"Pancreatic cancer. Doc Bailey says I might have six months."

Hawkins stares at the sign above the jukebox that reads Live Free or Croak. He looks at Ruby and says, "You look great."

"Thanks," Ruby says. "It's funny, I've never felt better."

"You still writing?" Ruby asks.

Hawk doesn't hear the question. He's studying Ruby and wondering if what people say about heredity is true.

Ruby's father and grandfather both required shock therapy.

"Every small town has its crazies and they're ours," Hawk remembers his mother saying.

But Ruby has never seemed crazy in a clinical way.

"I'm talked out," Ruby says, rising from her spot in the booth.

"You going?" Hawk asks.

"Yeah," Ruby says.

"Don't give up," Hawk says. "Doctors have been wrong before."

"I'm not giving up."

Hawk steps outside with her.

"What's next?"

"I'm going to see a fortune-teller."

"Why?" Hawk asks.

"To get a second opinion," Ruby says over her shoulder.

The List

1. Someone tall

2. ~~Good Looking~~ Attractive

3. Funny

4. Loves animals and the outdoors

5. Smart

6. But not an Ivy League graduate

7. At least not someone who's come a long way from an obscure Midwestern town to go to Harvard on a scholarship and who still—always—feels he has something to prove but can never live up to it and has to ever-so-subtly put you down, apparently because you only went to UC Berkeley, but more likely because he feels inadequate because his mother pushed him terribly hard to be more than his family members were and she never ever just accepted him for who he was

8. Not from a small town where they fry chicken in lard and pronounce Missouri "Mizur-ah" and look at you funny when you say you're from California

9. Has seen more than his own little neck of the woods

10. Likes to travel

11. World savvy

12. Sophisticated, a little suave

13. But not too suave. Or obsessed with sex. Not someone who flirts with everyone, seriously everyone—even the mannequins in the window display ("Whatchya doing after work, goodlookin?") at a high-end department store where he takes you swimsuit shopping because you were on the high-school swim team and he says he wants to see you strut your stuff and then he wears sunglasses at the indoor pool to hide his eyes and scrutinizes not only you but every other bikini too—and who greets all women with a kiss on both cheeks when he's not remotely French, and who, to top it off, dresses better than you

14. Someone down-to-earth

15. Friendly

16. Kind to strangers

17. But can keep his fly zipped. Who doesn't volunteer every day to walk the dog after work in the park across the street from your condo—without you so you can "rest a bit" from your stressful event-coordinator job—and then you see him through the window basking in the chick-magnet effect of a solitary T-shirt-and-jeans guy walking a freshly brushed and bouncy golden retriever

18. Trustworthy

19. Faithful

20. Honest

21. Has morals

22. But not religion.

23. At least not a fundamental cult-like religion where the people are oh-so-nice and at first he seems such the gentleman and you'd be happy to bring him home to your family, but it turns out his church doesn't let him date outside their own group, so he has to sneak around with you and is nervous all the time with a buzzing energy that is either guilt or excitement or both every time you get together and it's confusing and you're wondering what is his problem and you even ask him "are you married?" because you've had enough of the infidelity thing, and he laughs and says no and explains that he's devoted to God and has to be mindful of where worldly pleasures fit in, but then he's willing to rub up against you as if by accident with a hard-on that is beyond cucumber and more like a wood baton and he kisses you on the neck lingeringly and greedily and you think he's about to die with desire and then when you finally sleep together it's explosive and several times in a row and then the next time you talk it's only so he can tell you that he can't see you anymore because he's "re-devoting" himself to God, and you get the impression (though he doesn't say it outright) that he had to publicly confess and go through a shaming process

24. Someone who knows his own mind, is not a slave to group-think

25. Someone nonconformist, a little different, exotic

26. But not a Slovenian, or who claims to be but hasn't heard of Maja Novak, your favorite female Eastern European writer, and who has two passports with different names and photos that hardly look anything like him and he shrugs it off as funny, ha-ha, and says names sometimes get translated wrong and says he had to reapply and didn't send one back because he told them he lost it but then he found it again and the picture's funny because faces change when facial hair gets unruly, but you still wonder, and he receives phone calls at all hours in a language that could be Slovenian for all you know but sounds harsh and angry and he's shipping lots and lots of packages because he's in imports and exports, and you take one to FedEx for him and he says it's all just "this and that" when you ask what he exports, and then after a few nights with you at a cabana near La Jolla he disappears and then his phone is disconnected and you wonder what you might have been complicit in

27. Someone law abiding

28. Someone real

29. Someone who's been around the block a few times so he's patient and compassionate and suffered just enough to be kind and is willing to go out with a person with a pitiful relationship track-record because he realizes it's not all your fault and maybe he's been through the same kind of thing

30. But most likely someone who's given up on online dating, friend-setup dating ("I know a great person" dating), casual dating, serious dating, interracial dating, boy-next-door dating, intergenerational dating, pick-'em-up at the train-station dating, call-a-number-at-random dating, or is just plain taken because that's where all the good ones go

31. Doesn't drive a dark-windowed, inscrutable, black sedan, like the ones that have started circling the block

32. Someone who will probably never read a dating profile unless it's in another universe

33. Someone from another universe where it's possible to meet at the right time and place with mutual interests, and his flaws you can tolerate and he's patient with yours, and you have fun together even when you are doing nothing, but you also go on adventures, and he likes your family and you his, and even though you agree on many things you also challenge each other to see new viewpoints and to experience life in a brand-new way

34. Someone

STAN SANVEL RUBIN

The Limits of Computational Models

When conditions exist for damaging winds
you can go about your business, as they say,
forewarned and *forearmed,* keeping
your mind and body on track
as if it's just another day, but only
diligence plus luck can keep you safe
when hail the size of bullets hits the roof,
and the heart doesn't have a roof,
but shelters like an animal
in its burrow of memories.
I can be shamed by youth and strength,
and knocked off my socks by beauty,
which always surprises when it hits
like a force five tornado
sweeping everything away
in the moment it blows past,
but I am flattened by grief
which, like beauty, has a lot to answer for
if we could ever pin it down
and ask why this house collapses
in the relentless fleeting wind
and not that one.

SARAH RUSSELL

Leaving West Virginia

The road curls snug against the hills,
dips into hollows, rises up through stands
of oak, rough against dun clouds
that promise snow.

Old Jimmy waves goodbye, and Maude
is backlit in the door. Homesick starts here
on this gravel road, I guess—nuzzling deep
in sun-sweet quilts, an owl keeping himself company
at midnight, clanking the old stove to life
come morning.

The world is raw, waiting where the road
goes flat and blurs in a rush to get somewhere.
I watched for dawn this morning, breathless to be gone.
Now I want to salt away this place the way it is,
the way I was.

Double Shift

The diner glows fluorescent at 2 a.m.,
beckons boozers and truckers, runaways,
women between men.

Mary receives them
as her namesake received Gabriel,
pours coffee unbidden, tends
to coconut cream and lemon meringue,
eggs over easy, a malt for the guy
with stringy hair, jittery for a fix.

She saves her tips in a pickle jar
under the grill—enough, she hopes,
to post 50 bucks for her old man's bail
come morning.

Marriage

Never a Rolex,
never a full orchestra, never

a coaster under a cup,
not for love, or brilliance,

or bubble baths,
no Norco for the pain,

no wine sample,
no island cruise,

just two archaeologists
in the desert,

back to back,
brushing away the sand.

Hope, they never find
what they are searching for,

just sweat in their eyes,
and the occasional brush

of a gloved hand
across sunburnt skin.

Eddie P

Because his last name was a collision
of Soviet bloc consonants, co-workers
at the repair shop called him Eddie P.
He mocked his own habits and I took
that lesson. His crisply creased shirt
suggested an iron at home or a wife.
He wore short sleeves in winter, always
a necktie. During lunch hour he worked
crossword puzzles, conjuring a pencil
from behind his ear while grinning.
While I didn't want to be like him
I didn't exactly want to be like me.
When I left that job for good—
for what I thought was better—
Eddie P shook my hand goodbye—
then quickly flat-footed back to his desk
as if fate had cast all words and answers.
He liked durable things, whether gas ranges,
or those shoes that always served him well
in damp basements or alleys. He'd been
one of the guys—then his back went out—
but he still wore those shoes like appliances.

Birder's Guide

Look birders I love you but
you can keep your check-marked lists:
    shrike;
    warbler;
    vireo;
the wonders you've seen;
store them in a dusty drawer.

I keep returning to the old favorites:
    first robin of spring;
    bluebird on my shoulder;
    cardinal sin.

My mind's an amphitheater where
the startled heron swoops upward
into air, its crackling call
a blue-glazed vase in a well-fired kiln.

Why hope for impossible odds of:
    Black-Tailed Godwit;
    Graylag Goose;
    Yellow-Faced Grassquit?

In the face of change the harlequin
voice of the mockingbird adapts
by mimicking cell phone ringtones;
and when it comes to song, ever the ugly choir,
even now a flash mob of starlings
is making sweet gravel in the air.

Every Rising Tide

Day Zero:

Teddy watches it on the news, same as everyone else. The eye of the storm, its projected path, the little white buzzsaw rolling along the coast. He tells himself it is just another false alarm—what that pretty blonde anchor calls "nuisance flooding." The type that sends fresh Midwestern transplants scurrying inland over a couple inches of saltwater.

But he has his stubborn pride, and two glasses of gin blooming warm in his belly. He looks at the pictures on the wall, the lemon tree in the backyard, the kitchen door frame where his mother had marked his height each year with a ruler and a blue ballpoint pen, and he knows right away that he won't be able to let it go.

Teddy digs out the candles, the flashlights, the first aid kit. Thirty-six bottles of water in shrink wrap. He hangs binoculars around his neck—his lucky pair, the ones he'd used to spot a smooth-billed ani next to the airport. He feels prepared.

Day One:

When the first waves hit, he watches the muddy water come sluicing down the blacktop, bearing sodden newspapers and black, wet branches. It laps at the curb and starts its slow creep up the driveway.

It's not so bad, he thinks. In a few days the streets will be dry as a bone, and every-one will be back with their luggage strapped to their cars and sheepish smiles on their faces.

Then a fresh wave carries in the tigers.

They come in a roil of fur and fangs, tumbling over and under one another with their wide, drowning eyes and their heavy paws slapping oar-like at the water. There seem to be dozens of them, an impossible number of tigers churning in the tea-black flood. Teddy feels a thread of fear unspooling in the pit of his stomach.

Day Two:

Through the second-floor window, Teddy watches the doomed Animal Control officer. He looks like a mailman in his khaki shorts and long white socks. He slogs through knee-deep water, one finger hovering over the trigger of a hunting rifle, eyes flitting back and forth like he's at a tennis match.

The officer never sees it coming. A pair of tigers launch themselves from the side alley, clearing the distance between them in an instant. A scream cut short, more sur-prise than pain. The tigers hunch over their kill, snowy chins dyed red.

Teddy secures the windows, stacks furniture against the door. The phones are dead. The water is rising.

Day Three:

Floodwater is seeping under the front door. The welcome mat is swollen, ringed with silt.

They are scratching to get in. He raises the binoculars, settles on the remains of the Animal Control officer. A sickly-looking tiger is pulling at his half-eaten thigh, tearing away marbled chunks of flesh.

Teddy retches into the toilet, forgetting for a moment that he can't flush it away. He drinks a bottle of water and tries to ignore the hunger gnawing at his gut.

Day Four:

He wakes to a crash of crockery and stumbles blearily downstairs. One tiger in the kitchen, slinking around the counter. Another shouldering its way through the crack in the front door. He sees the shrink-wrapped case of water bottles in the sink, considers making a grab for them.

Their eyes are what frighten him. Pinprick pupils set in perfect golden orbs. Looking into them stakes him in place. Teddy feels like an insect pinned splay-limbed to the specimen board. He can smell the hot, coppery tang of blood on their breath, can hear the low growl at the back of their throats, like a furnace that is always being stoked.

He backs up slowly, up the stairs, remembering something he saw on one of those nature programs, about how tigers won't attack if you are looking right at them. Praying it is true.

He reaches the second floor landing and makes a break for it, up the waiting ladder and through the attic window. He scrapes his palms on the shingles, feels the binoculars pressing against his sternum as he climbs onto the roof.

He sleeps there, laid out in the still night air, looking up at stars scattered like birdseed. Wet heat clings to him, so thick that he can almost feel it weighing him down. He dreams of dripping mouths.

Day Five:

Teddy watches a water moccasin thread its way through the oily water. It has risen again overnight; tigers float along the street on mattresses, doors, an upturned clawfoot tub.

Their patience is tireless, atavistic. He won't outlast them.

Teddy turns over onto his stomach. There is a bottle of water bobbing like a lure in the current below, and for a feverish moment he casts his eyes skyward, as if someone might have dropped it there. He reaches for it, knowing before he does that it is far beyond his grasp. He laughs out loud, the dregs of good cheer drawn out of some hidden wellspring. Soon the laughter collapses into a strangled sob.

On neighboring rooftops, buzzards are already lining up to regard him with their raw, boiled-looking heads. Another clot of them wheels overhead, forming a lazy hangman's noose that Teddy knows is going to close around him, eventually.

He lies on his back and looks at them through his binoculars. He chews his cracked lips and imagines them growing larger and larger, the papery rustle of their wings transformed, swelling into the steady chop of a helicopter's rotors. He imagines it hovering overhead while he squeezes his eyes shut against the downwash. In his mind, it is all very heroic. There is the rescue crew in their bright uniforms, arms outstretched, smiling beneath mirrored shades. They will touch down on the roof, pull him aboard, swaddle him with blankets and offer him as much water as he can stomach, and at last he will smile back and wonder out loud what the hell ever took them so long.

ERIC SHATTUCK

Catch and Release

NOW, WHEN I THINK about my mother, the image that comes to me is her kneeling on the bedroom floor with the keepsake book, taking things out and arranging them in a semicircle in front of her: playbills, concert tickets, movie stubs, valentine cards. She kept every letter my father ever wrote to her, every note they passed back and forth in high school. Twenty years' worth. Even then, young as I was, seeing that dredged up this feeling—a perfect, fluttering knuckleball of heartbreak.

*

It was the summer my father finally taught me how to fish. He'd set up some kind of deal with the neighbors, gone in together on a pontoon boat rental for the weekend. We went out onto the lake armed with poles and a cooler full of cheese sandwiches and rum. My father bought me sodas at the bait shop and then spent the first fifteen minutes on the water making a pitcher of mojitos, squeezing the limes and muddling the mint by hand. He winked at me and said, if you were going to use mix, you might as well save your energy and just drink the rum straight.

My mother sat under the awning with the neighbor's wife, nursing their drinks while I learned how to tie on a hook. I made my father thread the worm onto it.

The first and last fish I ever caught was a perch, maybe as long as my hand. The hook had gone too deep, through the gills. When I pulled it onto the deck, it wasn't even fighting. Before that, I'd never stopped to think about whether fish could bleed. My father took a pair of needle-nose pliers and dug the hook out, tossed the perch back into the water, trailing bright red. Right away it rolled belly-up. "Shit," was all he said.

Afterward I sat in the front of the boat and looked out across the water, tracking schools of quicksilver minnows, or the box turtles that levered themselves off of the bank without a sound. I saw it the same time my mother did, I guess. My father brought the neighbor's wife another drink, and his fingers lingered on hers, as if they were the only two people in the world.

My mother fixed another drink herself, then put on a pinched smile, so that it seemed like wherever she looked, something amused her. But she wouldn't look him in the eyes. She drank quickly, like she was taking medicine. After the fourth refill my father walked over and covered her glass with his hand, and she kept pouring anyway, until he pulled away and wiped his fingers on his shorts.

And before they could start up again, before they found new words to wound each other with, I pushed myself away from the boat and into the lake. The cold took my breath away, but I paddled out as far as I could. And then, because it was the cruelest thing I could think of, I unbuckled my lifejacket and slipped my arms through the holes.

When they noticed me, that was when they started shouting. Just as I went under. It was strange, how different they sounded. The peculiar way voices carried underwater—not at all the way they did through ghost-thin drywall. I tried to hold my breath, my lungs feeling like they were about to crack, escaped air wobbling up to the surface.

I felt my father's hands under my arms, like the fish that feels the sudden heat of the hook in its cheek and understands. As I was pulled aboard I saw my mother, waiting to wrap me in a towel, the sun hanging low behind her and lighting her up like a Byzantine halo. Anger on my father's face, but alloyed with something like fear.

*

I am the one who finds her. Lying on her back, one arm hanging off the bed like a swimmer reaching for shore. Like a fish gone belly-up. The other arm draped across the keepsake book, the way a driver will throw an arm across the passenger seat before a collision, as if flesh and bone could stop what is coming.

She didn't leave a note. Or, she left many notes, but none of them were her own. I think of her on her knees, all of those letters and tickets arranged like wards against harm. What must it have felt like, to know that none of them could help? That you can sleep in the same bed and still be alone when the lights go out?

Glory

GLORY TO YOU, oh Lord. For calling your servant Harold Carter home this morning, glory. For the hours of his days and the days of his years, glory. For the love Harold gave. And the love he received. For the work he did. And the rest he earned...glory.

And thank you, Lord, for calling your servant Tonia, before this morning's light, to witness Harold's passing and to behold the lift of his spirit from this troubled world to peace in you at last. And for these old worn old hands of hers that held Harold's in his final moments and that you then allowed to bathe his body so that his children might see Harold cleansed in readiness to meet you, Lord. For all of this, praise and glory.

Dear Lord, may Harold's death not riven his children from whatever thin life in your spirit they might enjoy...I sense they are not godly people. His son seems so attached to his cell phone that it might as well have grown straight out of his skull. Even at the minute of his father's passing, he was in the hospital hallway. Calling his wife, he said, although I suspect his text messages definitely do not have a "wife-like" tone.

And, as for Harold Carter's daughter, well, she came every day to see her father. But always doused in duty, never in love outright.

Although they may not know it, Harold's children need you, Lord. So in their loss, fill them with your presence. In their sorrow, let them feel the comfort of your hand. And in the darkness of their grief, see the light of your grace.

Bless them, Lord, as I know you will bless all the people jammed together on the trains I hear rumbling behind me this fine morning, and as you bless the wide waters of the river running before me, even as I let myself rest on this bench before going home to wrestle an eyedropper full of kidney medicine into my old cat's stubborn mouth. And bless my daughter and grandbaby who are taking me to see *Disney on Ice* tomorrow.

And thank you for this morning of the fifth day, third week, sixth month, twelfth year of your servant Tonia's sobriety. Glory for that, Lord, glory.

And, Lord, as the river runs before me, I swear I can almost see Mr. Carter riding home to you on the rays of the morning sun. So, before he reaches your gate, please call my boy Tavon to your side to greet him.

Tavon was always up, eating, his cereal and watching cartoons when I got off work...you know that, Lord. And know how that boy always said, "How ya doin', Little Mama?" and then got out the door quicker that I could ask, "Where's your school books, Tavon?" In those days, me and Tavon passed like the uptown, downtown trains runnin' behind me. I knew he wasn't goin' to no school, Lord, but I was so tired and craved a drink so bad, I just let him run out onto the streets. And you know what the streets were,

Lord...you made them. Although I have to confess, I don't know why you made them so they ate up all those young boys like they did. So, please have my boy with you when Mr. Carter reaches you this morning.

Lord, in my sobriety, I live by the good book, and I believe the might of your word. And so I know your love has no limits and that you have numbered even the hairs on my head. So you know, Lord, how, since this early morning, my hairs have numbered one less. That one less being the one I plucked from my scalp and pressed into Mr. Carter's right hand. Washing and cleaning him, I sensed his spirit lingering—the ones who depart with scant faith do that, Lord. Unaccustomed to being so freshly freed from life's burdens, they're reluctant to leave. No longer sensing who and what they were, they stay a bit. Poor things, they need time to let go.

I sensed Mr. Carter was one of these reluctant ones, so while he was still nearby I asked him to give that one hair of mine to Tavon. And that's why, if you will, Lord, please have Tavon by your side when Mr. Carter reaches you: it would make handing over that hair a whole lot easier. I hope you agree, Lord, that a boy should have something of his mama's until her own time comes.

The only other thing I ask, Lord, is that you extend your mighty hand, the one that laid out the earth over which the train tracks run, and that cleaved the riverbed over which the waters tumble to the sea. Extend that hand, Lord, to your servant Tonia and keep your hand upon her while she climbs the stairs to her apartment and gets that medicine into her old cat's stubborn mouth. And, please, Lord, let her feel your hand upon her all the number of her days. Until they are all spent. And she comes home to you in Glory. Amen.

EMMALINE SILVERMAN

Questions About My Mother's Wild Years

Those poolside nights, when boys strummed
the Dylan songs that lived within your bones,
did you sway palm-like and sing along,
or like a recluse in a plastic chair,
hug your knees and sip the salted breeze
with notes of tanning oil and magnolias?

When the chalky pill began to glow
throughout your veins, were you the first
to twirl, too bright for clothes and stillness,
or did you locate water and a bed, and trace
the stitching of the coverlet a hundred times
and murmur at its silkiness?

Did you think the high would last? Or know
that California would amount in future years
to a strip of sultry greenery you glimpse
through linen curtains in the mid-Atlantic
while your solemn daughter asks the names
of every well-groomed flower in the yard?

As the only bender of my life (pills and penthouse,
Brooklyn Bridge at five a.m. in burnished light)
melted into afterglow, I thought of you
with reading glasses and a pensive frown
helping me complete my taxes.
I gathered questions I will never dare to ask.

DANNY EARL SIMMONS

On One Hard Father

—for Roger Weaver

Whenever frozen webs of sidereal dawn reflected white off the cold
winter moon, whenever warm exhalations were gray and socked in,
whenever all that existed between purpose and perpetuity was darkness

upon frost, whenever gloves and hat and thick blue flannel were not enough,
whenever the thermos in his right hand provided ballast against the frigid

slickness that stretched the length of the path connecting the kitchen door
to the lowing along the once red barn, whenever his left hand balled
into a tight round of responsibility and too many mouths to feed, whenever

Big Boy greeted him with 15-hands of mottled muscle and nostril-steam
prior to being led by small talk and habit to the leather bridle worn smooth

by one fulfilled obligation after another, he'd conjure a little extra warmth
from somewhere deep inside before breathing it slowly over Big Boy's bit—
out of consideration for his horse. My father was good with horses.

DANNY EARL SIMMONS

On Being Shunned at the Chinese Buffet Triolet

"do not even eat with such a person." —1 Cor5:11

It's all tough love and heat at the Chinese buffet
of sweet sour shunning, Kung Pao and fried rice.
Sunday's stiff wooden rulers no longer hold sway,
so there's tough love and heat at the Chinese buffet.

My old brothers and sisters hold hands as they pray,
Thank You, Lord, for The Truth, Dim Sum, and The Light,
It's all tough love and heat at the Chinese buffet
of sweet sour shunning, Kung Pao and fried rice.

Homesick

For the rages, the stories, the stair step
up to a small bedroom cast in cement,
for the anger welling up. Homesick
for a garden transplanted from Europe
to the harsh wastes of Winnipeg.
Heartsick for frostbite, waltzes, chocolates,
and crusted snow—to be a favorite of hers,
that grandmother who never befriended
the flatlands. For Streusels she refused to cook,
and roasts burnt to a crisp while she read mysteries.
What blood, what bone do I carry in my belly?
How many stories before Dachau,
and the few who are freed? Homesick
for the train whistle, its dreaded departure,
cars loaded with the stink of waste.

WILLIAM R. SOLDAN

Elegy for an Uncle (?)

HE WAS ALWAYS the one you took after, even when you were just a little shit who'd only visit in the summers, reveling in Grandma's material excess and how she'd spoil you kids rotten, while your mom stayed back in Ohio, in her own way reveling that she had one less mouth to feed for a couple months.

He lived in the basement with the pool table and the bar, the tacky wood paneling and rusty shag. Man, that was the place. That's where you learned to emulate a way of living. It got into your fibers, probably. Impossible to get out.

He took you with him and his girlfriend down to Milwaukee in his pickup truck, and on the way down let you shift and gave you your first taste of alcohol: the bottom third of a Bartles and Jaymes wine cooler. Strawberry. Like a revelation on your tongue.

When he got arrested on the lakefront—open container, public intoxication, drunken disorderly, something in the neighborhood, anyway—the girlfriend, curly brunette hair and stonewashed jeans, thin T-shirt the only thing between her mature flesh and your accelerated six-year-old desires, kept you in her care and you watched as the car drove off with him in the backseat, his face a half-and-half of guilt and something else.

And there was the time he bet you five dollars he could swallow a live minnow and puke it back up whole and wriggling. You were maybe seven or eight at the time. He did it, and you were too young to know not to take the bet because where the hell were you going to get five bucks? So to impress him you swallowed one, too, but couldn't muster the guts to finish the trick, and even now, when you think about it, you can swear you feel it swimming around in there just behind your belly button.

That was the same summer you went to Florida, the time just the two of you went "cruisin'" along the beach in Grandma's truck with Pink Floyd cranked to a bone rattle, and he taught you how to hang your wrist over the steering wheel and "check out babes" while a fresh-cracked Budweiser sweats between your legs.

But he could be scary. Little guy with a ten-foot temper, ready to take on the biggest sonofabitch in the room, even when it was only himself standing in his underwear in the parking lot of some Louisville motel while you were on our way back from Disney World, you and your little cousin watching as he screamed at the night and Grandma pleaded in her gravelly voice for him to *Jesus Christ please come back inside.*

He'd get that look in his brown eyes and you'd just know one had checked out and another had checked in. A look someone close to you not long ago described during one of those next-day salvage missions where debris was all you could retrieve from the previous night, before the lights went out.

But he always remembered to call on your birthday, on Christmas, even when he was locked up in the joint.

Twenty years later and you'd bring out the worst in each other. He'd share his meds and you'd do weird things like move the TV or rearrange the furniture in your sleep. You'd deny doing it but suspect it was you and vow never to mix brandy and Vicodin and Rozerum again, because no matter how much fun it might be to hang out at a bus stop with Abe Lincoln and a deep sea diver like in the commercial, there's just too much of the wrong kind of potential there.

Lacking control in life is one thing.

By then you knew he was dying, you all did, he had been for years. Nothing if not tenacious. The stalwart will of high tragedy housed in skid row architecture. But no one would take his calls.

And the thing is this: You think of your father's eyes—the ice blue of an arctic canine. Mom's green like soft moss. It's known to happen, yet you can't help but wonder, as you sort through what's been handed down, maybe your brown eyes aren't so special, after all.

The Arsonist: Fire Redux

Lord who crams the night with stars, who puts a path
in my way and floods it with embers.
I hear the intimacy of rising flame, a sigh like a homing
plane descending through a sinuous tunnel of sound,

hear it through my flesh. I strip away the burden
of choices, discard the personal, that never-quite-safe
as too costly and in defense would score the others with my
knife like an orange leaving them naked in their acrid

skin. Lord, what then is this intrusive sadness
I feel even in sleep and in the morning when I wake
into living, such glitterings of hostility? You direct the wings
of the guileless into pleasurable heights with loving tyranny,

but lead me, fettered stallion towards dry ground,
the non-sustaining pasture burned by the welding torch.
Lord, extend Your hand, loosen my fetters, and anoint me
with Your healing oil. I step in and eat.

PETER J. STAVROS

Three in the Morning and You Don't Smoke Anymore

IT'S THAT THING that wakes you at three in the morning, with a gasp and a startle, brain addled, pulse pounding, the pillow and sheets sweat-soaked. You roll over to the nightstand for a cigarette before you realize you don't smoke anymore, quit years ago, but it still remains, that muscle memory, to reach for something, no matter how toxic, when you sense yourself sinking. You unfold out of bed, this leg, then that leg, pause for a beat to acclimate to upright, sort of, before stumbling down the stairs, clumsy against the rail, the hardwood creaking, that one nail on the next to last step that always snags your sock, goddammit, boxers and V-neck damp, clingy. You check the air conditioner, running full blast, set at sixty-two. *Sixty-two?* You jump to adjust to something more sensible, seventy at least, the unit outside clanking off with a rattle of hard metal. *Christ, who set this thing at sixty-two?* You would never be so cavalier with the thermostat, and thinking like that makes you feel like your dad. You resist the urge to rummage through your desk drawer for a crinkled pack of Marlboro Lights that might have gotten shoved way in because even if it had it would have long been pillaged by you by now.

It's no use, you know, but you go to your desk nonetheless, something draws you, and the chair you stole from the last place you worked, those assholes who were too cheap to offer you severance. You had to take something for your time, so rather than abscond with a briefcase of office supplies like any normal person, or a wad of petty cash stuffed into your overcoat pocket, you took a shitty chair, rolled it down the hallway as security escorted you from the building. You never even liked that chair, the insufferable squeaking at the slightest shifting of position. But you had to take something. And now here it is, in your house, squeaking, squeaking, squeaking, as you sit at your desk, and open your laptop, for some reason, some reason that escapes, at three in the morning, your damp underwear. You log on, you log in, and there, then you remember, why you woke with a gasp soaked in sweat.

It's her, you see her, like you used to see her, older of course, what's it been, ten years, no, more, but still the same, sort of. You see those lips, those eyes, the button nose, the unruly shock of platinum blonde hair, not natural, not what God gave her, but suits her, the mermaid tattoo from Key West. It's her, you know it's her, older but still it's her, smiling, contented. She's standing on some anonymous beach, with some anonymous kid, some kid who looks like her. It's her kid, her son, they told you it's her son. *Is that really her son?* He looks like her and not his father whoever that is and why isn't he in the picture although you suspect maybe he took the picture but you would rather just consider him out of the picture. He's a good-looking kid, tall, towers over her, but she's small, you always teased, yet even so, a kid that big, and good-looking, with all her best features and nothing from his father whoever that is. You see that, you saw that, and still cannot believe it, and now you can't stop staring.

It's why everything that used to be you and her rewinds into place, sort of, grainy footage from another era: how she smelled, how she tasted, how she felt brushed up against you, soft and safe, how she pleaded that crisp autumn night right before she left if you would ever settle down and you could not articulate an answer to make her stay. You reach for your breast pocket for a cigarette but you don't have a breast pocket and you don't smoke anymore anyway, quit because of her, because she hated the smell, and what it did, and she wanted you to be healthy. You would go on those ridiculous long runs with her in the park, panting and coughing and struggling not to vomit, just to be with her, and you would pretend those runs were the best ever while secretly longing to lounge on the stoop inhaling deep satisfying drags from one of the stash of "cancer sticks," she called them, you managed to hide from her.

It's that thing that makes you wonder what the hell you have been doing with your life, these many years, while she was raising a good-looking kid with all her best features who towers over her. You, sitting in your damp underwear in a shitty chair you stole from those assholes who fired you for no other reason than they didn't want you there anymore. You, in the same place you have always been, at this starter home you bought when you first moved into town, and here you are, still not started. You resist the urge to pull on a pair of sweats and wander down the street to that gas station with the buzzing neon beer signs that never closes for a pack of something and a bottle of something only because you don't want to go to the trouble. Instead, you sigh, shut the laptop, rise from the chair, squeaking, squeaking, squeaking, and slurp two handfuls of water from the bathroom sink, splash what's left on your face, then head upstairs, to bed, toss the pillow and peel off the sheets, lie on the mattress, the plastic covering sticking to your moist skin, grabbing slightly and releasing with every heavy breath. All you want is to fall asleep, to be done with this day and endless night, because tomorrow might be different, better maybe. Tomorrow you might do something.

Just Do

THE ZOO SMELLS like popcorn and animal dung. We're standing in front of the Capuchin monkeys and watch as children stick twigs and little fingers through the fence. My boyfriend has his arm around my waist, tight, like a cramped muscle. He is chewing gum and smacking and popping the neon green goo right by my ear. I feel him looking at me, but I don't look at him. I'm here only because I want to see monkeys and pandas and he promised that he'd drive.

My boyfriend makes me banana pancakes in the morning and takes care of my bills. He rubs my shoulders when I'm tired. He hums lullabies when I can't sleep. He says he's the best I'll ever have and that I can't leave. Mom says thirty-three is too old not to be married. My sister tells me never to settle. Dad says I better start freezing my eggs, and I say I don't know I don't know I don't know.

We're still watching when a brave monkey ambles over to us, hooks long, limber arms through the fence and hoists itself up to our level. I cock my head, and it cocks its head, blinks intelligently at me through beady eyes.

"He's looking at me," I say.

"Nobody's looking at you." My boyfriend says this a lot, even when we're alone. He says it so much that I hear it when he's not there. He says it and I believe it.

The children are throwing rocks at another monkey, one who's perched on a clump of dirt next to the water bowl. The monkey just sits there and takes it, like this is what's expected, like this is all it's ever known, and I have the awful feeling that if given the choice to leave, the monkey would choose to stay.

I'm overcome with an urge to go home. "Can we leave, please?"

My boyfriend scratches his beard. "Not yet," he says. His jaw slides from left to right, and then he smiles, like he takes pleasure in denying me things, which might be true. Sometimes he says other things that I believe. Like, the reason why I had to drop out of college: Stupidity. The reason why I never walk on sidewalk cracks: *Stupidity*. He says these things with clarity and concision. His words could cut through steel.

I start towards the children to tell them to stop throwing when my boyfriend spits his gum into the cage, the monkey on the fence converging on it the way blood runs down a needle. It scoops up the neon green lump like water and chomps until it disappears.

"What'd you do that for?" I ask.

My boyfriend laughs but no sound comes out. His head tilts back and his mouth hangs open like a hooked fish.

It's moments like these where I think about tempting disaster, like not wearing a seatbelt, or driving too fast. I think about buying prescription drugs off college students and Jack Daniel's from the liquor store. I think about telling my mother I don't love her and biting my fist for lying. But at some point I need to stop thinking, and just *do*.

The monkey chews and chews and chews but I'm hoping he will keep going, and that he will still be chewing for the next five, ten, twenty years because I don't want to know what happens when he swallows.

DANIEL J. SUNDAHL

St. Joseph's Field: Abbey of Gethsemani

The hurricane spread across the coast
Has made the brothers thoughtful,
Their faces more far away than usual.
They know but will not pander God's name.

By ones and twos they walk through the wet grass;
Other men have come for surrender and remorse,
The fragile cargo of their scudding boats
Somehow having shifted, wavering on the ocean's face.

Another man, small in size, walks
Beside the Abbey's walls; he stops by an opening;
He takes a freshly sharpened ax, quartering pine.
Jet trails hook a loose embroidery in the sky.

Clearly a little permission is a dangerous thing
In these times when no one has a clear conscience.

DANIEL J. SUNDAHL

Thoreau in South America

The words and notes tell of Brazil;
The orange and purple swell of fruit,
Red bird in green pine, a flash of flicker,
A dwelling on the word tanager, a mystified swing
Of words and notes paying for themselves in wonder.

*

I put dry wood inside the burner.
I wish for something warm and slow and good.
My own father, dead now nearly thirty years—said nothing
Of value except *here is life, don't waste it, don't fail.*
I imagined this morning the odor of loblolly and bay.

*

Without the possibility of loss I am non-existent.
I walk across my neighbor's land; the deer
Have left instructions, directions. Hippocrates,
You write, *has even left instructions how we should cut
        our nails;*
*That is, even with the ends of the fingers, neither shorter
        nor longer.*

My own nails are short; I feel sad and foolish.
My own pond is dark, saturated with weeds.
Flurries come from the west; a stray goose gropes south.
I turn to go home, a place of equable temperature,
My own house a sort of entrance to a burrow.

*

Delight, I read, *knows its season;*
Related to cumulus vapor it fills the abyss.
In black jungle trees the means to invent
Compassion spreads green Mayan feathers;
The high leaves speak to an unheard presence.

Foreclosure

My father was sledgehammer
running into walls.
My mother, the sheet rock,
taped and textured and painted
to keep the insides of the house from showing.
They sparked the rock with alcohol.

From my room at two a.m., I heard,
hole by hole, the house come down.
Outside a monster made of string
circled through the neighborhood,
screaming the skies fell down.
Through the window I smelled
gas fields on its breath.

Plaster was a remedy for fools.
Everyone that came after
always felt and noticed still
the outline of those holes my father made.
Men like him, thousands,
leveraged into blunt objects, the women,
crumbled to foundations.

Water Cycle

My father kept his secrets under the surface of himself.
When he finally tore them out one morning
before the fog had cleared
he rowed to the center of a lake
somewhere west of town
and dumped the secrets overboard.

That's the story my mother told
a thousand times the same.
She left out the part about my father
ripping fragility from his veins
that same veiled morning.
He must have hoped to drain his way to the sea.

We felt evaporation true,
the depths of the distance between them
from the wreckage and the silt
to the ripples on the surface of clouds.
On nights when it would thunderstorm
we'd let the raindrops melt into our tongues.

Turn Left at the

tree at the edge of the street that wears lovers'
initials in her chest. Four faded letters cut

beyond the bark, into the very brown of the thing.
Yesterday there was an old man, maybe

in his sixties, staring at the oak through
the haze of his cigarette. Watching the initials

as if they would re-create themselves
into something more honest. I wanted to ask

are you HF? I thought *HF* was the blonde
boy who died in Afghanistan six months

ago. As part of a convoy to some city where death
is as commonplace as fornication. I thought

HF and *KP* broke up when she walked in
on him kissing the waitress we all admire. The old

man stepped out his cigarette, drew his collar
and moved into and beyond the puddle of

yellow cast on the pavement by a streetlight.
They hid the blonde boy's body in the rainy ground

at the Catholic cemetery and the local senator came
and told us how great he was. How the business

in Afghanistan wasn't really his and that he died
for his country. They gave him a flag and a full name.

KP didn't come back because she was in Portland where
she sells flowers from the window of a shop. Her initials

still linger at the end of my street. Sometimes
someone we know will use the tree as a landmark but

mostly it just stands at the end, haggard,
just outside the streetlight's glow.

Our Windows Are Dusty Photos

The things that are happening here—
fried eggs, magpies, rain,
huckleberry and dollar drinks,
are the strange results of mountains.
The black creek, the brick bars,
the space that sheds rivers,
and the valley we call home
are veils, chance fates no longer lured
by long roads out of town.

And we love it. The familiar drifts
of pine, drenched aspen aged by
wind, sparrows splayed across
lilac yards. Rainy gutters.
The sighing fence.

Our lives breathe here. Our sleep
is good. We walk along where rivers
start. In the shaky distance, the moon
glows above abandoned tracks.
All day our windows are dusty photos
of the distance we've crossed.

Moving West

I lean into November
running around the country
quietly looking for people I used to know
in places they used to live.

Greeley, Colorado, on a Sunday: the space
between campus buildings
is full of cold spring walks.

I trace the thatched contours of three years,
the soft collage of prairie roads
that led me away from home.

Along damp riverfronts
where I once looked forward to my life,
young cottonwoods have grown—
mimicking a mountain's breeze.

Whim delivers its blows
to this town named after a man
who promised young men
new lives out West.

I am running behind their legend.

I am trying forgiveness
for places that release the people
I love. There will never be

another spring so cold
or so long ago.

ERIC TWARDZIK

Fruitcake

I WAS ASHAMED of my conscience. I'd never done anything like it before. But I'd just gotten back from my mid-morning run and it was waiting in the hallway of my building, a brown cardboard package with "Collin Street Bakery" stamped in old-fashioned letters on the side and addressed to "Mrs. Marlene Donaldson" via a sticker on top.

A fruitcake. From Texas. That's what I stole from the octogenarian lady upstairs. An octogenarian lady who was by all accounts very sweet and fully deserving of respect and a certain polite form of pity, who I'd met many times and occasionally visited to fix her printer or set up her DVR. And now I was sitting at home, in bed, in my underwear, using my bare hands to eat the Christmas confection her daughter had sent her.

Not that I like fruitcake. Far from it. But I figured that I had to eat a good portion of the thing. Chunks of pineapple got lost in my sheets.

So that was the start. In the weeks leading up to Christmas I took more boxes from the hallway. Always after my mid-morning run, when everyone else in the building would be at work, practicing medicine or law. I'd take the plunder upstairs—I was loathe to imagine myself stuck in an elevator with another resident, holding their package ("Why, I was just about to bring this up to your place, Mr. O'Connor!)—mounting the steps two at a time.

There were clothes. Mostly women's—it seems that the wives of the building did all the online ordering. I'd begun wearing a lemon J. Crew cardigan originally meant for Janet Steiner downstairs, a woman built big enough so that the sweater wasn't a bad fit. The best part about the plundered clothing was that I couldn't give a damn about what happened to it. I fixed myself spaghetti and meatballs, and streaked the sweater red as I twirled strands of pasta with my fork.

There were books. Mostly of the dull and expected variety, self-help or thrillers, but I did manage to find a tome titled, *We're Worth It: A 10-Step Guide To Saving Your Marriage Together* addressed to the Nielsens. I half-hoped to discover *Mein Kampf* in someone's Amazon package, but nothing that exciting ever happened.

Everything else defied easy categorization. Child-sized shin guards. The wine-of-the-month. A globe that opened up and became a wet bar. My new belongings occupied more and more of the studio apartment, until I could no longer see the floor and had to carve a dedicated lane running from the door to my bed to the bathroom.

Sometime in January I heard a knock on the door. I pulled off the two-sizes-two-big cashmere sweater I'd been wearing (Mr. Lindquist, fourth floor), threw on a white T-shirt and opened the door to the slightest crack I could manage. There stood Janet Steiner, looking puffy and red, probably from the ordeal of climbing two flights of stairs.

179

"I just wanted to let you know that there's been a rash of stolen packages in the building," she said, "and we're going to have a meeting to address it tonight in my unit."

I nodded along. She lowered her voice and continued.

"I think it's the Vietnamese man that cleans the basement."

Later that day I rented an SUV and parked it a block away from the building. I waited until 3:30 a.m.—I had set an alarm—and then started taking everything out. Expensive olive oils, mohair socks, ceramic salt-and-pepper shakers, Panini presses. They all went into the car.

But I didn't stop. After I'd taken out all the plunder, I took my own clock down from my kitchen wall. I removed my flat-screen TV from the cabinet. I dis-assembled my IKEA coffee table. I gathered up all the photos of Anna and I, which still lined the windowsill for some reason, into my arms like kindling. It all ended up in the SUV, where they rolled and writhed on the floor with the material debris of strangers. I drove until I found a dumpster behind a forsaken-looking pizzeria and emptied the contents of the SUV inside.

Now my apartment was empty. No trace remained from my weeks of thievery or the life before it. As I sat on my bare mattress and contemplated the white wall before me, I realized that I was finally free to go.

Heavy Compulsion

TENSION AND TEN heavy girls play Barbooth in the projects while it rains in unholy sheets outside. The shooter casts two miniature dice and throws two threes and wins. Mona Lisa's pet cat crawls underneath the furry olive-colored table and snuggles up to Boot Baby's leg. Boot Baby kicks the feline, furious that Harley Charley didn't throw a one and a one, or a two and a two, or a four and a four, or a one and a two; because if he had, she would have won. Like the others, Boot Baby had five dollars on that stupid roll and if only those two little cubes would have revealed something good. A two and a two would have been great, she thinks, as the rain pounds against the window.

Boot Baby doesn't know any of the other girls and she doesn't care. She knows they all live around here somewhere, and after the game, they'll all go back to where they came from, most likely busted, disgusted and not-to-be-trusted. The game's dice man, Harley Charley, allows Mona Lisa to bring her black-and-white cat to his daily Barbooth game because he doesn't mind cats and it makes Mona Lisa Baby happy. "I aim to please," is his motto and Harley Charley doesn't own a Harley-Davidson motorcycle—but he looks like he might—that's how he got his neat nickname. He has a beard and always wears a leather jacket and chaps to his dice games.

So Harley Charley throws another round, a six and a six, and he wins again. Boot Baby takes a snort of her absinthe and lets out a huff. The other nine heavy girls also lose. The roller has thrown wins for himself over a dozen times in a row and the ten heavy girls are beginning to think his Barbooth game is rigged.

"Do you have somethin' in those dice?" Mona Lisa asks him.

"Nope. It's all in the wrists," the dealer says.

"You've got loaded dice, Harley Charley," Mona Lisa complains.

Harley Charley wheezes, takes a toke off his unfiltered Pall Mall, and shows his ochre-colored teeth, not in a benign smile, but an evil grimace. His smile's more like a rictus—and Boot Baby cringes at Harley Charley's unholy-looking physiognomy.

"It's an old Middle-Eastern dice game and almost anything can happen," Harley Charley explains. "It really helps if you're Jewish or Greek. None of you ten heavy girls look like you're part of either ethnic group."

So the girls all get out their little pocketbooks and each fishes for another five to throw on the table. A stack of fives growing like a skyscraper of currency is now situated in front of Harley Charley. His weekly dice game is a hit around Barleycorn Estates, a place filled with heavy girls, their heavy kids, along with their heavy significant others (it's amazing how heavy Barleycorn Estates is with heavy people).

"Bones to the loan, let 'em roll," Harley Charley wheezes, and spins a 6-5 and he wins again. He stretches out his long skinny arm and like a net, waves it over the fuzzy green table top, pulling in all the fives.

"Bones to the loan, go to fucking hell!" Boot Baby screams.

"Cool down girl. It's all for fun and entertainment. Just shits and giggles," Harley Charley laughs.

"When's this stupid game over?" Paradise Alice asks, finagling a toothpick around between her two sharp-looking incisors.

"It's over when all you heavy girls lose all your heavy fives," Harley Charley says.

"I just won't come in Apartment 27 anymore," Hunchback Hilda says, snorting down her whiskey and water like an old schoolmarm drunk on a dare on the bad side of Omaha on the last night of a science teachers' conference.

"Back to the wall, let 'em fall," Harley Charley wheezes, and rolls a 2 and a 2, and the girls are overjoyed that all ten of them will be able to split Harley Charley's five stake—for fifty cents each. But after the two square soldiers seem to settle on the table, those blasted bongs boomeranged, revealing a 3-3 combo.

"So nice doing business with you heavy ladies," Harley Charley wheezes, and stretches out his skinny arm, netting all nine fives in one vast sweep.

"I can hardly wait until this game is over," Mousy Moose mentions. Mousy Moose clocks in at a hefty 657 pounds. And on a five-two frame, that's a lot of heavy girl to cart around on those big, fat heavy legs and feet. Mousy Moose is the lightest and the sveltest of the group—that's why she got the nickname Mousy Moose. Her christened name is Babalonia Breathoff, by the way, and she's retired (and loving it, she says on Facebook) from a factory that manufactures dog, monkey, and cat food.

"You nine can walk out of Apartment 27 any ole time," Harley Charley says. "And you know the drill. My daily dice game starts at 1 p.m. sharp and lasts, well it lasts until I have everybody's fives and everyone leaves Apartment 27 frowning."

"You're a bastard, Harley Charley," Mousy Moose snorts.

"Yes I am. I am indeed," he answers and rolls another 1-1 combination and does the usual. His arm is beginning to get tired from all the stretching—but it's a labor of love for him.

"I can hardly wait until this game is over," Mona Lisa complains.

"You can pick your fat ass off your little ole chair any time you please," Harley Charley huffs. "And you know if you want to come back again tomorrow, I'll be here, in Apartment 27 with my dice again tomorrow. It starts at 1 p.m. sharp. And it's always very local—in wonderful, fabulous, fabled Barleycorn Estates."

"I'd leave but I just can't," Boot Baby sighs.

"I can't neither," Hunchback Hilda whispers.

"Ah, you ladies have to lighten up. It's all for fun. Shits and giggles and cyanide tablets covered in honey," Harley Charley says as the rain pounds on the only window, and it seems to be getting a lot heavier and hungrier with each cast of Harley Charley's set of dice.

DONNA VITUCCI

Muslin Prayer Book

MY SON, MY SON. The threads inside you hold their breath. Old wives tails and tonics—what I wouldn't try to spare you, cure you, set you free. My charge, my skinny-minnie boy-twig, why won't you eat? Or rather, why won't what you eat stick?

The doctor says the worm has you, sends us to the pharm where the glass bottles cast colors across his wood floor. Aisles of remedies on display, but wouldn't you know I have to name it to buy it, and then the druggist he calls it out loud so all the shoppers may shame me. What's wrong with my home that such nasty should root in? Is where we live such filth? No! I'm a good mother, good housekeeper, clean woman. My children have the usual snot under the nose and grub beneath soft fingernails.

They play, friends, they have curiosity, they create worlds in the make-believe bush and jungle out in the alley and walk-behinds, the bloody boardwalk where drunks and pissers make deals. My son doesn't haunt the dark, yet the dark haunts him. He eats but remains stunted and wan.

And now he's been prescribed the vermifuge. Hail Dr. McClane, he knows how and why. He's brewed the elixir to rid you, darling, of your ills. The spoonsful chased by buttermilk. Swallow, swallow, I'll stroke your throat. There, now.

I've read the advertisement cards, the testimonials. The ferret, the nasty rat-hunter, nasty as the rat himself, he circles the hole in the foundation. Beady-eyed cousins who eat their own. Foul world stacked on foul world, mirroring this tenement. And we presumed we were higher, like birds on the branches, out of reach, lofty, even above the apes. But we and apes both have nits, and birds pluck up worms, so the cycle is complete. See, my child, doesn't the blue bottle cast the prettiest bow when we hold it like this up to the light?

*

Doctors instruct and we don't question. Done as he said, followed with a piece of licorice to swab at the white coating your tongue. You cry, but you are ever sniffling over the odd and dangering prospect, too much fire or too much water. Wait for the boiling and then we'll add ginger and cayenne, the leaves I picked by the stoop. You can never learn this too soon, darling: everything's useful if we take it into us.

The muslin crushes under your kicking legs. Tis true, this lap has known softness and the wet, but when you take into your head to beat me you do it well, you do it until the muslin and I flinch from the blows. My mother assured me once the babies came I would have them forever, something at last for me alone, to love me alone, and here, my boy, you end up raising the devil in these walls. Off-kilter. Unsettled. Creeped and goose pimply.

I wish his remedy would douse your spiking, but there's the pillow and the afore-mentioned fire if all else fails. The escapes I can reckon help me weigh you through the night and count on morning coming the way it breaks like an egg or a stone straight to the head. Knock me out, Lord, and tear this boy from my arms before bad I can't take back strangles these fingers and all they touch. For I am muslin, thin to see-through, ghost of an apron, the world glancing through, and my boy, he shimmers on the other side of me like flint set against the sun.

DONNA VITUCCI

Ward

I only remember waking up here. How long have I been?

Such a blessing she doesn't remember the grand-girl who knuckled her to her own kitchen floor over a purse with four dollars in it, also a gummy collapsible rain hat, lint ridden lozenge, and a raft of grandchildren school photos 1985 through 1994. Look at the blonde baby's snarling metal mouth, studs punctuating her soft ear parts and nostrils, and fingernails bit-to and bleeding as they fight over the pocketbook. The old woman had swallowed nothing but canned cold tomato soup for three days; it was easy for her fingers to cede their grip.

The girl just wanted to feed her monster. Her granny's love was a clouded window in a Barbie dream house Christmas lost. She'd been loved easily but love no longer mattered. Her granny's love was snow screen on an old television set, granny rendered small and ineffective, and by her own flesh and blood. She was a ladybug stuck to the sill of the window while the girl flew past the metal in her body with the speed of sleek promoted aircraft, and catastrophe soon to rage in the acceleration, in the powerful smoke and ash. And the granny eye to eye with a Frosted Flake against the kickboard beneath the sink. The woman conjured up sugar and stale grain, the gush of spit to surround and soften it, her jubilant tongue melting once the grand-girl shed her.

Does this place have sweeteners for our coffee?

Sunday Meeting

Stone-still under the sun.

A sudden caress, cool and kind
as a young mother's kiss
on the top of a baby's head—and gone.

Cataleptic heat again.

What meteorological madness
goes to the trouble of creating these tender airs,
artfully braiding five directions at once,

then cancels them with the flick of an off-switch,
causing the bird congregation to go silent
along with the rest of us hill residents,

except for Father Crow

in his Cotton Mather weeds, squawking
fire and croaking brimstone, mad as hell
and determined to wake up every sinner,

sloth and saint in these red cedars?

ANNA LOWE WEBER

Before you had a name

Bone-man I called you. I called you blink,
belly shudder, tag-along. Weren't you a minnow

then, swimming against the stream? I called you
mine but that's a laugh, right? A spinning yarn,

the story all parents wear like a hairshirt—close
to the skin and constant in its hurt,

a bleat you can't unhear. Listen to the lie—the way
it goes on, kvetching in the night. Even at your smallest,

a clump of cells in bloom, proliferation in rapid time lapse—
even then, the fibs you told were real whoppers.

I'm yours. I'm yours. Grow me right
and I'll never leave you.

Idiom

I feel the familiar chill of limestone
on my skin when he says
I'm an easy dog to hunt with.
I know he isn't from Arkansas,
doesn't drive a '91 Bronco with broken
turn signals, has never been swimming
in West Fork creek. He does carry a gun,
but it's not the twelve-gauge that rusted
in my living room closet
during the winter of '04.

All I can say is *I lived in the Ozarks,*
but he doesn't understand.
He only sees mountains and trees,
not the November day when that truck,
the gun, an Arkansan boy, and me
went up on Sugar Mountain to look
for turkey. It was a minor accident,
a mishandled turn that launched us

into an oak. I was wearing my seatbelt,
but the boy wasn't and his head made
a thumping sound when it struck the wheel.
The loaded gun fell out of his lap,
but didn't fire. It wasn't until
I picked it up later that I saw
he'd already turned off the safety.

Nighthawk

In the dim half–light,
you live again.
A soaring nighthawk,
you circle above me,
the day's grief
swirling and retreating
with the swoop of your wings.
You fly between
the full moon and me,
and the light flickers
in waves and strips,
like a reel of film
reaching its end.

JOHN SIBLEY WILLIAMS

Oklahoma City, Oklahoma

A bustling dance hall is one kind of loneliness.
The arms of strangers linked and guiding
my body through song
after song. Terrifying release. Unbelonging
of togetherness. Light as I stamp it
into sawdust and hay. Bourbon. Fiddle.
Tomorrow's bright white pews filled or
emptied of organ. As if I don't deserve either,
hold me,
steady me; love, after this nameless damp body of night, return me
that silence of waking
and waking alone.

JOHN SIBLEY WILLIAMS

Gettysburg, Pennsylvania

Like something too closely held to understand,
this field. And for the first time
since my christening my father is weeping.
Is this the god people talk about at night
when they've finished talking?

Only if they exhume every inch of bone
that fastens my great-great-great-grandfather to my femur
will I get to ask
how much of the field is really ours.

Big Sur, California

Breast-beating, continuous storm.
Storm that drives the towns further inland,
drives the seals from the rocks, deeper.
At our backs
lightning stitches up the sky, tries to heal, as
the ghosts we took for angels begin to itch
again.

Can you tell me where it aches?

Please show me on this emptied spiral of a shell
where the sea has touched you.

Hold me close to your ear. Yes, just like that.

Can you hear our folding,
our breaking against the coast?

PAUL WILLIS

Dry Creek

—Ross Lake Natural Recreation Area

Dry Creek, that you are not.
        The trail walks a checkered log
across your rapids. Yesterday
        I stood in the snow where you began,
white as the foam that courses
        now through moss, through boulders,
under the cedars and the hemlock
        to the gray, impassive lake.

I think I am alone with you
        until a young man rounds the bend
above the crossing—one leg flesh
        and bone, one leg sprung steel—
and he treads the log without a pause.
        His pack appears to be no burden.
He is heading, he says
        to me, for Desolation.

PAUL WILLIS

Desolation Peak

—Ross Lake Natural Recreation Area

Jack, I owe you an apology. Some years
ago I left a note on Matterhorn Peak:
Jack Kerouac is a weenie. All those
tributes to you and Snyder overflowing
the register—I couldn't stand it, what with your being
out of shape and hung over and not even making the top.
But today, sweating up switchback
after switchback from the shores of Ross Lake
through fog, through rain, through hail,
through drifts, through blow-downs and through
shredded boots, my hat is off to you in the wind
as I sit on the doorstep of your lookout,
gazing across the dam-drowned Skagit
to the darkness of Mox Peaks,
the ones described by Fred Beckey
as a good place for a funeral.
That's you, Jack. Your moxie to be up here
for two months and more before you died.
I was wrong: you're more than twice the man
I thought. The clouds are closing in again
and it's starting to snow. I'm out of here.

MARTIN WILLITTS, JR.

Boat of Names

*Tōrō nagashi is a Japanese ceremony in which participants
float paper lanterns (chōchin) down a river on the last evening
of the Bon Festival*

1.

I write your name on a paper lantern
to guide your spirit to the *other* world,
the one without pain or need.

I set it on the river. From water to water,
I return your name.

2.

The river takes the name to a world of paper.
The paper is folded into a lantern
lighting the way. A spirit knows water
carries many voices; none of them
remember pain.

Pain remembers
it could wrinkle a person with fear,
turn blood into pulp and sawdust.

All the words sit in ceremony.

3.

Out on the ocean, sky,
more sky, sky without land
beyond the reach of seagulls,

there is no home, no goodbyes—
either it is water that is moaning
or it is the boat following the currents
without a destination
no more than a cloud has a care
where it goes.

The boat slips into the sky
headed towards the bewildered,
intense as a lover.

It feels like riding on the back of a seagull.

CODY WILSON

Redding to Phoenix

I carry splinters
from her backyard patio
chair where I peeled the skin
of paint off the cracked wood
920 miles south and across
state lines; my arms
harbor a piece of her

porch. Now she sits shotgun
in my mind, and when I roll
down the glass, receipts fly
in circles. I mix my hand
through the whirl—I catch
a fast food napkin,
and because it's all that's left,
I wipe my face. I reach

toward the streaming
highway, that napkin
fluttering furious below
my thumb. When I let it
go, it flashes once, white
in my mirror, and is gone.

CODY WILSON

What I See in You I Don't Know

Your hip to rib ratio is almost even.
My hand dives the dunes of your torso,
the twist of your spine as you lie

on your side. You are sand. An hourglass
full. There is no time left in you.

When I was young and just learning
how to swim the butterfly, we were told
to draw you on the pool's bottom,

an hourglass portrait on the plaster, sometimes
a keyhole, once, when I was old enough
to hear it, *a woman's body:*

Feel the silhouette drag
through your hands. Push it down, toward
hips, thrust into it. Breathe and repeat.

This is how I learned to swim,
how I learned to breathe between suffocating
myself for the sake of your figure.

I never thought of sand
in that hourglass, never
of a key to that keyhole,

never your body to that outline,
but now all I see is: a glass full of sand,

a key that doesn't work, your back
as you face the window instead of me.

Lord How It Would Ring

Richard Smith

Bill Monroe was tall.
He had a temper.
He learned how
to finger-pick
from a black man
named Arnold Shultz,
who walked off
into the dusk,
singing.
Monroe tried
to enforce the order
of his creation—
picked notes flying
like tiny butterflies
that can't be caught.
He was unreformed
as Yahweh, full
of wrath and sentiment.
I am who I am
said the thing in the tree,
the bush burning,
the hug-eyed child
who grew up shy,
feeling his way
through a world
of sound (creak
of hinge, Mama
singing, his own
voice an angel
yell behind the clay-
cutting plow).

His mama died hard,
trying to walk off
pain. Her fiddle was
carefully kept.
Ten years earlier
she had played
the mandolin
all through a hot
summer day,
big with the baby
who would become
Bill, the raw chop
of her Gaelic tune
transubstantiated
into bluegrass—
a stylized cascade
like Mondrian's ocean
or the staccato
of loom and piston.
Her boy slap-dashed
off Uncle Pen's hill,
riding the roads
of Jim Crow America,
the improvised infinity
of jazz hanging
like dust in the air.
Out of that holy grit
strode Bill, our
motherless child,
full of venom,
spitting honey.
He would not abide
this poem, but
hold on a minute:
the wind sings
another song.
All our dead
gather around us,
just like he said.

Let My Child Run

*—from a reader comment on a New York Times story about
school shootings and the practice of lockdowns*

Across wide fields,
down hallways
of waxed linoleum,
over the reflected light
of gymnasium floors.
Let her run while
our good dog
scouts ahead,
tail a happy flag.
Our bodies are made
for such delight,
legs stretching out
with loving speed.
And, if the time comes,
should she run
instead of wait
behind desks
turned into shields?
I have a first grader
in America today.

The Woman Ages

as her chickens lay: as a matter
of course, without much trying.

She ages in defiance, asks
do you want to buy my soul—

this polar expedition, a net for
wolves, this desert in my teeth?

She's halfway to a wreck
or roadkill, the scat of God.

All she has to do now is fall
off the rung and land right-side up.

Holy Night

She thrusts her fist toward a hollow sky, gathers dirt around saplings newly planted, flails a ribbon through an Earth Day moon. She won't pray on nights like this—too raw, and carnal somewhere—too uncertain. But she'll bask in dog pack howls and coyote cries, and dream of younger days. She'll squat on an old concrete block and wait for the void to seize her like a holy fire.

CONTRIBUTOR NOTES

David Adès is a Pushcart Prize-nominated Australian poet living in Pittsburgh since 2011. He has been a member of Friendly Street Poets since 1979. He is the author of *Mapping the World* (Friendly Street Poets / Wakefield Press, 2008), commended for the Anne Elder Award 2008, and the chapbook *Only the Questions Are Eternal* (Garron Publishing, 2015). David was a volunteer editor of the Australian Poetry Members Anthology, *Metabolism*. His poems have appeared widely in Australia and the U.S. in publications, including over 20 of the Friendly Street Readers, and numerous literary magazines and have also been widely anthologized, most recently in *Verse Envisioned: Poems from the Pittsburgh Post Gazette and Works of Art They Have Inspired.* In 2014, David was awarded the inaugural University of Canberra Vice-Chancellor's International Poetry Prize and was also shortlisted for the Newcastle Poetry Prize.

John Amen is the author of five collections of poetry: *Christening the Dancer, More of Me Disappears, At the Threshold of Alchemy, The New Arcana* (with Daniel Y. Harris), and, most recently, *strange theater* (New York Quarterly Books). His poetry, fiction, reviews, and essays have appeared in journals nationally and internationally, and his poetry has been translated into Spanish, French, Hungarian, Korean, and Hebrew. In addition, he has released two folk rock CDs: *All I'll Never Need* and *Ridiculous Empire.* Further information is available on his website, johnamen.com. He founded and continues to edit *The Pedestal Magazine* (thepedestalmagazine.com).

Diana Anhalt, originally from Mexico, is the author of *A Gathering of Fugitives: American Political Expatriates in Mexico 1947-1965* (Archer Books), three chapbooks— among them *Second Skin* (FutureCycle Press) and *Lives of Straw* (Finishing Line Press) —in addition to essays, short stories and book reviews in both English and Spanish. She placed first in the Georgia Poetry Society's contest for their annual collection, and her work was nominated for this year's Pushcart Prize. Her book, *Because There Is No Return* (Passager Press), released in August, is now in its second printing.

Grace Arenas is an MFA candidate at the University of Montana. Her chapbook, *they'll outlive you all,* is forthcoming from Dancing Girl Press in late 2017. Her work has previously appeared in *Thank You For Swallowing* and *Pretty Owl Poetry.*

Pamela Arlov is a teacher and a writer. Her poetry has appeared in *Pine Mountain Sand & Gravel, Ekphrasis, Parody,* and *The Blue Hour,* among other publications. Her textbooks, *Wordsmith: A Guide to College Writing* and *Wordsmith: A Guide to Paragraphs and Short Essays,* are published by Pearson and are now in their sixth editions. She lives in Macon, Georgia, and teaches at Middle Georgia State University.

John Bate is a long-time English teacher at Montpelier High School in Vermont. He is interested in the intricacies of poetics and mystified by the elemental impulse that is the core of any good poem.

John Baum's work has been published in *Blue Mesa Review, Booth, The Saint Ann's Review, The Charleston Post & Courier, WhiskeyPaper, Jellyfish Review,* and elsewhere. Currently at work on a novel and a collection of short stories, he lives in Atlanta. Contact him at www.johnpbaum.com, @johnpbaum.

Sandy Beaches has been writing for over 20 years. She grew up in Boston with her family and a variety of small cats. This is her first publication.

Christopher S. Bell has been writing and releasing literary and musical works through My Idea of Fun (myideaoffun.org, an art and music collective based out of Johnstown, Pennsylvania) since 2008. His sound projects include Emmett and Mary, Technological Epidemic, C. Scott and the Beltones, and Fine Wives. Christopher's work has recently been published in the *Madison Review, Red Rock Review, Quail Bell Magazine, Commonline Journal, Mobius, Gesture, Crack the Spine, Foliate Oak, The Gambler,* and *Eclectica* among others. He is also a contributor to *Entropy*.

Dick Bentley has published fiction, poetry, and memoir in over 260 magazines and anthologies on three continents. His books, *Post-Freudian Dreaming* and *A General Theory of Desire,* are available on Amazon. His new book, *All Rise,* contains poems and short stories, plus samples of his inventive "wall poetry"—poems that are displayed as part of paintings and graphic art. These works have been shown in collections and art galleries. Dick has served on the board of the Modern Poetry Association (now known as the Poetry Foundation). He's a Pushcart Prize nominee and was prizewinner in the Paris Review/Paris Writers Workshop International Fiction Awards. Before teaching writing at the University of Massachusetts, Dick was Planning Director for the Boston Housing Authority. He is a Yale graduate with an MFA from Vermont College.

Roy Bentley is the author of four collections of poetry, including *Starlight Taxi* (Lynx House: 2013), which won the 2012 Blue Lynx Poetry Prize; *The Trouble with a Short Horse in Montana* (White Pine: 2006), which was the winner of the White Pine Press Poetry Prize in 2005; *Any One Man* (Bottom Dog Books: 1992); and *Boy in a Boat* (University of Alabama: 1986), which won the 1985 University of Alabama Press Poetry Series Award. Recipient of a Creative Writing Fellowship from the National Endowment for the Arts, six Ohio Arts Council fellowships, and a Florida Division of Cultural Affairs fellowship, he has taught in colleges and universities in Ohio, Wisconsin, Florida, Iowa, and New Jersey.

Carol Berg's poems are forthcoming or in *DMQ Review, Sou'wester, The Journal, Spillway, Redactions, Radar Poetry, Verse Wisconsin,* and elsewhere. She has three chapbooks, *Her Vena Amoris* (Red Bird Chapbooks) and *Ophelia Unraveling* and *The Ornithologist Poems* (dancing girl press). She received a grant from the Massachusetts Cultural Council.

Nancy Bevilaqua's poems have appeared in or are forthcoming from *Up the Staircase Quarterly, West Branch, Stirring, Hermeneutic Chaos, Whiskey Island, Atticus Review,* and other journals. In late 2014, she published a poetry collection entitled *Gospel of the Throwaway Daughter*. She is also the author of *Holding Breath,* which is a memoir of her experiences as a caseworker for people with AIDS in the 1980s. She hopes to publish her long poem, *Gelyana,* as a chapbook in the not-too-distant future. Born in New York City, she now lives in north Florida with her son.

Lisa Lynn Biggar received her MFA in Fiction from Vermont College. She is currently marketing her first novel, We Were Here. Her short fiction has appeared in numerous literary journals, including *Litro Magazine, Bluestem Magazine, Newfound, Main Street Rag, The Minnesota Review,* and *The Literary Nest.* She teaches English at Chesapeake College and is the fiction editor for *Little Patuxent Review.* In her spare time, she co-owns and operates a cut flower farm on the eastern shore of Maryland with her husband and four cats.

Ace Boggess is the author of two books of poetry: *The Prisoners* (Brick Road Poetry Press, 2014) and *The Beautiful Girl Whose Wish Was Not Fulfilled* (Highwire Press, 2003). His writing has appeared in *Harvard Review, Mid-American Review, Atlanta Review, RATTLE, River Styx, Southern Humanities Review* and many other journals. He currently resides in Charleston, West Virginia.

Carl Boon lives in Izmir, Turkey, where he teaches courses in American culture and literature at 9 Eylül University. His poems appear in dozens of magazines, most recently *Burnt Pine, Two Peach, Lunch Ticket,* and *Poetry Quarterly.* He is also a 2016 Pushcart Prize nominee.

Bethany Bowman is originally from New York's Mohawk Valley. She lives with her husband and two children in Indiana, where she teaches at the local high school. Her poems have recently appeared in *Ascent, Blueline, Midwestern Gothic, Lime Hawk,* and *Relief,* and are forthcoming in *Nimrod.*

Charles W. Brice is a retired psychoanalyst living in Pittsburgh, PA and is the author of *Flashcuts Out of Chaos* (WordTech Editions, 2016). His poetry has been nominated for a Pushcart Prize and has appeared in *The Atlanta Review, Chiron Review, Fifth Wednesday Journal, SLAB, Sport Literate, The Paterson Literary Review, The Pittsburgh Post-Gazette, Spitball, VerseWrights, The Writing Disorder,* and elsewhere.

Caleb Busch was born in Milford, Massachusetts, and is currently enrolled at The New School in New York. He has been previously published in *Litmus Magazine.*

Wendy Taylor Carlisle lives and writes in the Arkansas Ozarks. She is the author of two books and four chapbooks, most recently *Chap Book* from Platypus Press, UK. For more about her work, check her website at www.wendytaylorcarlisle.com.

Michael Carrino holds an MFA in Writing from Vermont College. He is a retired English lecturer at the State University College at Plattsburgh, New York, where he was co-founder and poetry editor of the *Saranac Review.* His publications include *Some Rescues* (New Poets Series, Inc.), *Under This Combustible Sky* (Mellen Poetry Press), *Café Sonata* (Brown Pepper Press), *Autumn's Return to the Maple Pavilion* (Conestoga Press), *By Available Light* (Guernica Editions), and *Always Close, Forever Careless* (Kelsay Books). as well as individual poems in numerous journals and reviews.

Michael Catherwood's recent or forthcoming publications include poems and essays in *The Minnesota Review, New Plains Review, The Galway Review, Plainsongs, Bluestem,* and *Louisiana Literature.* He is an Associate Editor at *Plainsongs.* His first book is *Dare* from The Backwaters Press. His second book, *If You Turned Around Quickly,* was published in June 2016 by Main Street Rag. His third book, *Projector,* is forthcoming from Stephen F. Austin Press in spring 2017.

Sara Clancy is a Philadelphia transplant to the Desert Southwest. Her poems have appeared, or are forthcoming, in *The Linnet's Wings, Crab Creek Review, The Madison Review, Antiphon, Verse Wisconsin, Turtle Island Quarterly, VAYAVYA* and *Houseboat,* where she was a featured poet. She lives in Arizona with her husband, their dog and a 23-year-old goldfish named Darryl.

Clayton Adam Clark lives in St. Louis, his hometown, where he works for Health Literacy Missouri, a nonprofit that helps healthcare organizations simplify their communications so more people can get good care. He also volunteers as an editor and board member for *River Styx* magazine. He earned an MFA in poetry at Ohio State University and is currently seeking publication for his first full-length collection. Some of his other poems are forthcoming in *Harpur Palate, Southern Humanities Review,* and elsewhere.

Grant Clauser is the author of two poetry books, *Necessary Myths* (Broadkill River Press, 2013) and *The Trouble with Rivers* (Foothills Publishing, 2012). Poems have appeared in *The American Poetry Review, The Good Men Project, Painted Bride Quarterly, Southern Poetry Review* and others. He also writes about electronics, teaches poetry at random places and chases trout with a stick. His blog is at uniambic.com.

Joan Colby has published widely in journals such as *Poetry, Atlanta Review, South Dakota Review, Gargoyle, Pinyon, Little Patuxent Review, Spillway, Midwestern Gothic,* and others. Awards include two Illinois Arts Council Literary Awards and an Illinois Arts Council Fellowship in Literature. She has published 18 books including *Selected Poems* from FutureCycle Press, which received the 2013 FutureCycle Prize; and *Ribcage* from Glass Lyre Press which has been awarded the 2015 Kithara Book Prize. Three of her poems have been featured on *Verse Daily* and another is among the winners of the 2016 *Atlanta Review* International Poetry Contest. Her newest books are *Carnival* (FutureCycle Press, 2016) and *The Seven Heavenly Virtues* (Kelsay Books, 2017). Colby is a senior editor of FutureCycle Press. Website: www.joancolby.com. Facebook: Joan Colby. Twitter: poetjm.

Gayle Compton is currently employed as an office flunky but has worked as a substitute teacher, coal miner, radio announcer, and general greenhorn in the steel mills and sweatshops of Detroit, Michigan, and East Chicago, Indiana. He got his English degree from Pikeville College and Morehead State University; he is therefore self-taught. Having spent time both in church and in jail, he finds one as comfortable as the other. His often satirical stories, poems, and essays on the Appalachian experience have earned him many awards and public aspersions. Compton raises cats and hell in Pike County, Kentucky.

Julie Cox is a lifelong Kentuckian and has taught English for fifteen years. When not writing or teaching, Julie enjoys alt-country music and shopping in used bookstores. She lives with her husband and children in south-central Kentucky.

Ken Craft is a middle school teacher and a writer living west of Boston. His poems have appeared in *The Writer's Almanac, Verse Daily, Gray's Sporting Journal, Off the Coast, Spillway, Slant, Angle Journal of Poetry, The High Window,* and numerous other journals and e-zines. *The Indifferent World,* his first poetry collection, was released in 2016 by FutureCycle Press.

Daniel Crocker is the author of a novel, a short story collection, and three full-length collections of poetry. His newest chapbook, *The One Where I Ruin Your Childhood,* is a free download at Sundress Publications. He teaches at Southeast Missouri State University.

Barbara Daniels' book *Rose Fever: Poems* was published by WordTech Press and her chapbooks *Black Sails, Quinn & Marie,* and *Moon Kitchen* by Casa de Cinco Hermanas Press. Her poetry has appeared in *Prairie Schooner, WomenArts, Mid-American Review, The Literary Review,* and many other journals. She received three Individual Artist Fellowships from the New Jersey State Council on the Arts.

Holly Day has taught writing classes at the Loft Literary Center in Minnesota since 2000. Her published books include *Music Theory for Dummies, Music Composition for Dummies, Guitar All-in-One for Dummies, Piano All-in-One for Dummies, Walking Twin Cities, Insider's Guide to the Twin Cities, Nordeast Minneapolis: A History,* and *The Book Of,* while her poetry has recently appeared in *New Ohio Review, SLAB,* and *Gargoyle.* Her newest poetry book, *Ugly Girl,* recently came out from Shoe Music Press.

Lori DeSanti received her MFA Degree from Southern Connecticut State University. She is the recipient of the 2014 William Kloefkorn Award. In 2015, she was a Feature Poet at Erbacce Press. Her work has appeared in journals such as *Paddlefish, Adanna, East Coast Literary Review, Winter Tangerine Review, Spry* and the 2014 Writer's Digest *Poem Your Heart Out* Anthology. She is the author of the poetry collection, *Saltwater Under Brittle Sky* (Swimming with Elephants Publications, 2015).

Patricia Duffaud is half French and half Northern Irish. She lives in London, where she is working on a novel, and her short stories, non-fiction and reviews have appeared in a variety of literary magazines, including *Wasafiri* and *Litro.*

Mike Faran spent his childhood in the UK. After his return to California, he served a four-year stint in the USAF and then went on to graduate from Cal State Fullerton. His poetry has appeared in *Over the Transom, Rattle, The Comstock Review, Abbey, Ship of Fools, Atlanta Review,* and *Homestead.* He is the author of *We Go To A Fire* (Penury Press) and is a Pushcart Prize nominee.

Marc Frazier has widely published poetry in journals, including *The Spoon River Poetry Review, ACM, Good Men Project, f(r)iction, Slant, Permafrost, Plainsongs,* and *Poet Lore.* He has had memoirs published in *Gravel, Autre, The Good Men Project, decomP,* with others forthcoming in *Evening Street Review* and *Cobalt Review.* He is the recipient of an Illinois Arts Council Award for poetry and has been featured on *Verse Daily.* His book, *The Way Here,* and his two chapbooks are available on Amazon as well as his second full-length collection, *Each Thing Touches,* which has been widely and favorably reviewed. His website is www.marcfrazier.org.

Paul Freidinger is a poet residing in south suburban Chicago. He has published over 200 poems in journals from all over the U.S and abroad. He has poems recently published or forthcoming in *Atlanta Review, Basalt, Bayou Magazine, Big Muddy, Cold Mountain Review, Confrontation, Folio, Florida Review, Grist, New Plains Review, Pacific Review, Santa Fe Literary Review, South Carolina Review, South Dakota Review, Still Points Arts Quarterly,* and *Triggerfish Critical Review.*

Amy Strauss Friedman is the author of the chapbook *Gathered Bones Are Known To Wander* (Red Bird Chapbooks, 2016). Her work has appeared or is forthcoming in *The Rumpus, Pittsburgh Poetry Review, FLAPPERHOUSE, decomP, Lunch Ticket,* et al. Amy is a regular contributor to the newspaper *Newcity* and a staff writer for *Yellow Chair Review*. She earned her MA in Comparative Literature from Northwestern University and now lives in Denver, CO. Her work is at amystraussfriedman.com.

Joy Gaines-Friedler teaches creative writing for non-profits in the Detroit area, including the PCAP (Prisoners Creative Arts Project) through the University of Michigan and Springfed Arts. A Pushcart nominee, her work has won numerous awards and is widely published in over 50 literary magazines and anthologies, including *Poetry East, San Pedro River Review,* and *RATTLE*. She is the author of two full-length books of poetry, *Like Vapor* (Mayapple Press) and *Dutiful Heart* (Broadkill River Review Press). A third book, *Control Theory,* is forthcoming. Joy did her graduate studies in American Renaissance Literature and holds an MFA from Ashland University, Ohio.

D. G. Geis lives in Houston, Texas. His first full-length book, *Fire Sale,* is forthcoming from Tupelo Press (Leapfolio) in February 2017. His chapbook, *Mockumentary,* will be published in September 2017 by Main Street Rag. Most recently, his poetry has appeared (or is forthcoming) in *Fjords, Skylight 47* (Ireland), *A New Ulster Review* (Ireland), *Crannog Magazine* (Ireland), *The Moth,* (Ireland), *Into the Void* (Ireland), *The Naugatuck River Review, The Tishman Review, Drylandlit, Permafrost, Gingerbread House, Damfino, Ink and Letters, The Worcester Review, Broad River Review,* and *Under the Radar* (Nine Arches Press UK). He was a finalist for the 2016 Main Street Rag Chapbook Competition, The Edna St. Vincent Millay Prize, The 2016 Louis Award, The 2016 Rash Award, and was shortlisted for the Percy French Prize (Strokestown International Poetry Prize Ireland).

A. Joachim Glage lives and writes in Los Angeles, where he is also sometimes an attorney. "The Empty Space Where The Future Is" is an installment in a series of fictions Glage is writing on the topic of human happiness (and its unsuspected evils); other works from this series have appeared or are forthcoming in issues of *Santa Monica Review, Philosophy and Literature, The Indianola Review, F(r)iction, The Pennsylvania Literary Journal,* and *Driftwood Press*.

Bill Glose is a former paratrooper and author of three poetry collections, including *Half a Man,* whose poems arise from his experiences as a combat platoon leader in the Gulf War. Now a full-time writer, he undertakes intriguing pursuits—such as walking across Virginia and participating in a world-record-setting skinny dip—to write about for magazines. In 2011, he was named the *Daily Press* Poet Laureate. His poems have appeared in numerous journals, including *The Missouri Review, Narrative Magazine, Poet Lore,* and *Atlanta Review*. His website (BillGlose.com) includes a page of helpful information for writers.

Richard Mark Glover has published short stories with *Oyster Boy Review, Bookend Review* (Best of 2014), *Crack the Spine,* and *Buffalo Almanac,* and he has won the 2004 Eugene Walters Short Story Award. His journalism has appeared in the *San Antonio Express News, West Hawaii Today, Ke Ola* and the *Big Bend Sentinel,* where he won the 2010 Texas Press Association Best Feature Award, medium-sized weekly.

Benjamin Goluboff teaches at Lake Forest College. In addition to his scholarly writing Goluboff has placed imaginative work—stories, poems, and essays—in many small-press journals. His collection, *Ho Chi Minh: A Speculative Life in Verse, and Other Poems*, will appear this year from Urban Farmhouse Press. Some of his work can be read at www.lakeforest.edu/academics/faculty/goluboff.

David Gross lives on a small farm near the Shawnee National Forest in southern Illinois and is the author of four chapbooks: *Cup of Moon, What We Never Had, Because It Is* and *Pilgrimage*. He has recently published poems in *Big Muddy, Blue Collar Review, Cape Rock, Common Ground Review, Hummingbird, Kentucky Review, Naugatuck River Review* and *Solitary Plover*.

Originally from New Jersey, **Madeleine Grossman** is currently a student at NYU studying English, French, and Creative Writing. This is her first publication.

Yen Ha is a principal at Front Studio Architects in New York City. Her work was a Top 25 finalist in *Glimmertrain*'s Short Story New Writers Contest and has been, or will be, published in the *Chicago Quarterly Review, Kentucky Review, Minola Review,* and the 2017 *New Rivers Press American Fiction* anthology. Her drawings and makings can be found at hh1f.com.

Miranda Haney is a student at Salisbury University working toward a bachelor's degree in Spanish and communication arts. This is her first publication.

Nathaniel Heely is a graduate of the University of Arkansas. He is currently an MFA Fellow in Creative Writing at Chapman University in Orange, California. His work has previously appeared in *Full Stop, decomP, Burrow Press Review, MARY: A Journal of New Writing, theNewerYork,* and several others. For more, visit nathanielheely.com.

Natalie Homer is an MFA candidate at West Virginia University. Her poems have been published in *Punchnel's, Santa Clara Review, Roanoke Review, Epigraph Magazine,* and elsewhere.

Robin Dawn Hudechek has an MFA in creative writing, poetry from UCI. Her poems have appeared in *Caliban, Cream City Review, Chiron Review, Poemeleon, Silver Birch Press, The Hummingbird Review, Inlandia: A Literary Journey,* and elsewhere. She has two chapbooks: *Ghost Walk* (the Inevitable Press, 1997) and *Ice Angels*, published in *IDES: A Collection of Poetry Chapbooks* (Silver Birch Press, October, 2015). Robin lives in Laguna Beach with her husband Manny and two beautiful cats.

Mike James lives and works in Chapel Hill, NC, with his wife and five children. His poems and reviews have appeared in numerous magazines, such as *Negative Capability, Chiron Review, Tar River Poetry, Birmingham Poetry Review, Iodine,* and *Soundings East*. The most recent of his eight poetry collections, *The Year We Let The House Fall Down*, was published last year by Aldrich Press. A new collection, *Peddler's Blues*, will be published later this year by Main Street Rag. He has previously served as an associate editor at Autumn House Press and as a Visiting Writer-In-Residence at the University of Maine, Fort Kent.

Richard Jones is the author of seven books of poems from Copper Canyon Press, including *The Correct Spelling & Exact Meaning*. His newest collection is *King of Hearts* (Adastra Press). Editor of the literary journal *Poetry East* and its many anthologies, including *Paris, Origins,* and *Bliss,* he also edits the free worldwide poetry app, "The Poet's Almanac."

James A. Jordan received his BA from Centre College, and is currently pursuing his MFA at the University of New Orleans. The recipient of the Cantrell Prize for Poetry and the Mike and Frieda Mullins Scholarship from the Hindman Settlement School Writer's Workshop, his work has appeared in the *Aurorean, Birmingham Arts Journal, Broad River Review, San Pedro Review, The Saturday Evening Post,* and *Town Creek Poetry*.

Artemis Journey is seventeen and insane, as Ray Bradbury put it. She is in a support group with a German shepherd and a black lab puppy, but all they really do is take naps and go hunting in the backyard for big sticks. She has been writing since she could read, and "Clubhouse" is her first published piece. Artemis dreams of becoming a Hobbit, moving to New Zealand, and never having to wear shoes again.

Charles Kell is a PhD student at The University of Rhode Island and editor of *The Ocean State Review*. His poetry and fiction has appeared, and is forthcoming, in *The New Orleans Review, The Saint Ann's Review, Poetry Quarterly, Eunoia,* and elsewhere. He teaches in Rhode Island and Connecticut.

Robert Lee Kendrick grew up in Illinois and Iowa, but now calls South Carolina home. After earning his MA from Illinois State University and his PhD from the University of South Carolina, he held a number of jobs, ranging from house painter to pizza driver to grocery store worker to line cook. He now lives in Clemson with his wife and their dogs. His poems appear in *Louisiana Literature, South Carolina Review, Kestrel, The James Dickey Review, The Sow's Ear Poetry Review, Main Street Rag,* and elsewhere.

Richard Krohn has spent most of his life in the Mid-Atlantic, but with substantial periods of time in the Midwest and Central America. He presently lives in Bethlehem, PA. His most recent work has appeared in *Poet Lore, Southern Poetry Review,* and *Rattle,* among others. He is always eager to engage with readers and other poets at krohn.richard@gmail.com.

Jennifer Lagier has published ten books and chapbooks and in literary magazines. She taught with California Poets in the Schools, co-edits the *Homestead Review,* and helps coordinate monthly Monterrey Bay Poetry Consortium Second Sunday readings. Her forthcoming books are *Harbingers* (Blue Light Press) and *Scene of the Crime* (Evening Street Press), and her website is jlagier.net.

Charlene Langfur is a Southern Californian, an organic gardener, and a Syracuse University Graduate Writing Fellow. Her writing has appeared in *The Stone Canoe, The Adirondack Review, Valley Voices, South 85 Journal, Earth's Daughters,* and *Spoon River Poetry Review,* and recently in a series of poems in *Poetry East* and *Weber—The Contemporary West*.

Rustin Larson's poetry has appeared in *The New Yorker, The Iowa Review, North American Review, Poetry East,* and *The American Entomologist Poet's Guide to the Orders of Insects*. He is the author of *The Wine-Dark House* (Blue Light Press, 2009), *Crazy Star* (selected for the Loess Hills Books' Poetry Series in 2005), *Bum Cantos, Winter Jazz, & The Collected Discography of Morning,* winner of the 2013 Blue Light Book Award (Blue Light Press, San Francisco), and *The Philosopher Savant* (Glass Lyre Press, 2015).

Daniel Lassell is the winner of a William J. Maier Writing Award and runner-up of the 2016 Bermuda Triangle Prize. His work has appeared recently or is forthcoming in *Slipstream, Atticus Review, Hotel Amerika, Split Lip Magazine, Reunion: The Dallas Review,* and elsewhere. He grew up on a llama and alpaca farm in Eminence, Kentucky. Today, he lives with his wife in Fort Collins, Colorado.

A native of Norfolk, VA, **Alex MacConochie** is currently pursuing a PhD at Boston University in Renaissance drama. His poetry has recently appeared in *The McNeese Review*.

Elizabeth McMunn-Tetangco lives in California's Central Valley where she works as a librarian. Her poems have appeared previously in *Kentucky Review, The Potomac Review, Word Riot, Hobart,* and *Right Hand Pointing,* among others. Her chapbook, *Various Lies,* is available from Finishing Line Press.

Tim Mayo's poems and reviews have appeared in *Barrows Street, Narrative Magazine, Poetry International, Poet Lore, River Styx, Salamander, San Pedro River Review, Tar River Poetry, Web Del Sol Review, Verse Daily,* and *The Writer's Almanac*. His first full-length collection, *The Kingdom of Possibilities,* was published by Mayapple Press in 2009. His second volume of poems, *Thesaurus of Separation,* was published by Phoenicia Publishing (Montreal) in 2016. A six-time Pushcart Prize Nominee and two-time finalist for the Paumanok Award, Mayo lives in Brattleboro, VT.

Anderson O'Brien lives in Columbia, SC. She has published poetry in numerous journals, including *The Iodine Poetry Journal, Blue Fifth Review,* and *Red River Review*.

Charles O'Hay is the author of two poetry collections, *Far from Luck* (2011) and *Smoking in Elevators* (2014). His work has appeared in over 125 literary publications, including *New York Quarterly, Cortland Review,* and *Gargoyle*.

Marlene Olin was born in Brooklyn, raised in Miami, and educated at the University of Michigan. Her short stories have been featured or are forthcoming in publications such as *The Massachusetts Review, Upstreet Magazine, Steam Ticket, Crack the Spine, Poetica, The Water Stone Review, The Broken Plate* and *The Saturday Evening Post*. Marlene recently completed her first novel.

William Page served four years in the US Air Force before earning advanced degrees in Tennessee and Ohio. He taught for the state universities of Texas, Alabama, Ohio, and Tennessee, retiring from Memphis State University, where he was a professor in the Creative Writing Program and Founding Editor of *The Pinch*. Page's poems have appeared widely in such reviews as *Kentucky Review, North American Review, The Southern Review, Ploughshares, Sewanee Review, Southwest Review, Rattle,* and *Wisconsin Review* and in a number of anthologies. His third collection of poetry, *Bodies Not Our Own,* won a Walter R. Smith Distinguished Book Award. His newest collection, *In This Maybe Best of All Possible Worlds,* won the 2016 FutureCycle Poetry Book Prize.

Jared Pearce teaches writing and literature at William Penn University. Some of his poems have recently been or will soon be shared in *Gyroscope, Harbinger Asylum, DIAGRAM, Fieldstone Review,* and *Infinity's Kitchen.*

Michael Phillips has published short stories and poems in several journals, including *Tar River Review, Roanoke Review, Philadelphia Stories,* a n d *The Monongahela Review.* He works as an editor for a nonprofit healthcare research institute and lives with his wife and baby daughter in Pennsylvania.

Cathy Porter's poetry has appeared in *California Quarterly, Harbinger Asylum, Chaffin Journal, Plainsongs, Homestead Review,* and various other journals. Her poem, "Clocked In," was nominated for a Pushcart Prize. She has two chapbooks available from Finishing Line Press: *A Life In The Day* and *Dust And Angels.* Her new chapbook, *Exit Songs,* was released in 2016 by Dancing Girl Press. She serves as a Special Editor for the journal *Fine Lines.* She lives in Omaha, NE.

Ken Poyner often serves as unlikely eye-candy at his wife's powerlifting meets. His latest collection of brief fictions, *Constant Animals,* can be located through links on his website, kpoyner.com, and on Amazon. He has had recent work out in *Analog, Asimov, Poet Lore, Sein Und Werden,* and several dozen other places, both in print and on the web.

Ana Prundaru is the author of two poetry chapbooks: *1L4S3T* (Etched Press) and *Unstable Tales* (dancing girl press). Her work is forthcoming from *velvet-tail, CALYX, Softblow, Lotus-Eater* and *Thread Literary Magazine.*

Clela Reed is the author of four collections of poetry. Her full-length books are *Dancing on the Rim* (Brick Road Poetry Press, 2009) and *The Hero of the Revolution Serves Us Tea* (Negative Capability Press, 2014); chapbooks are *Bloodline* (Evening Street Press, 2009) and *Of Root and Sky* (Pudding House Publications, 2010). She has had poems published in *The Cortland Review, The Atlanta Review, Valparaiso Poetry Review, Caesura Literary Magazine, The Literati Review, Storysouth Journal, Clapboard House Literary Journal,* and several others. She has recently returned from Peace Corps service in Romania, during which time she wrote weekly in a blog, clelainromania.blogspot.com. She lives and writes with her husband in their forest home near Athens, Georgia.

Ron Riekki's books include *U.P.: a novel, The Way North: Collected Upper Peninsula New Works* (selected by the Library of Michigan as a 2014 Michigan Notable Book), and *Here: Women Writing on Michigan's Upper Peninsula* (May 2015, Michigan State University Press). He's had eight nominations for the Pushcart, Best of the Net, and Best Small Fictions. His screenplay, *The First Real Halloween,* was selected as best screenplay in the sci-fi/fantasy category for the 2014 International Family Film Festival.

Larry Sherman Rogers is a singer-songwriter, poet, and fiction writer. Growing up, he lived in Berkeley and Compton, California, for a while but was mostly raised in a potting-shed trailer in the piney woods of west central Arkansas. He is married and the father of two grown children. He currently lives in Fort Smith, Arkansas, with his wife and four (at last count) cats. His songs have been published and/or recorded by several well-known artists in the music industry. Larry's poems have appeared in *The New York Quarterly, The South Carolina Review, Rattle, Pearl, Wormwood Review, The Chariton Review, A Clean, Well Lighted Place, Hanging Loose, The San Pedro River Review,* and *The Denver Post.* He co-authored, with Charles "Jenks" Norwalk, a short novel about war experiences titled *American Youth in Asia.* Songwriting partners, Charlie and Larry served together in Vietnam.

Anne Ross has published work in the *Berkeley Poetry Review* and written copy for Taproot Foundation. She currently writes regularly with an informal but dedicated writing salon where she is working on a young adult sci fi novel and every genre of flash fiction. Anne also creates artwork using found objects and alternative photographic processes. She works and creates in Oakland, California.

Stan Sanvel Rubin's fourth full collection, *There. Here,* was published in 2013 by Lost Horse Press. His third, *Hidden Sequel* (2006), won the Barrow Street Book Prize. His poems have appeared in many national magazines, including *The Georgia Review, Kenyon Review, Iowa Review, Florida Review* and others, and are currently forthcoming in *The National Poetry Review, Red Savina Review,* and *Poetry Northwest.* He lives on the Olympic Peninsula of Washington state and writes annual essay reviews on poetry for *Water-Stone Review* out of Hamline University in St. Paul, MN.

Sarah Russell has returned to poetry after a career teaching, writing, and editing academic prose. Her poetry has appeared in *Red River Review, Misfit Magazine, The Houseboat, Shot Glass Journal,* and *Ekphrastic Magazine,* among others. Her poem, "Denouement," won the Goodreads poetry contest in February 2014. Follow her work at SarahRussellPoetry.com.

Logan Seidl is a graduate from the University of Nevada, Reno. Recently, he has won the DQ Award in both fiction and poetry, and the James H. MacMillan Scholarship for poetry/fiction written about Nevada. His poetry has been published in *Crack the Spine, Constellations,* and *The Meadow.*

Dave Seter is a civil engineer and poet. Originally from Chicago, he currently lives in Sonoma County. His poetry and critical works have recently appeared in *Paterson Literary Review, Evansville Review, Palaver, Confluence,* and other journals. He received his undergraduate degree from Princeton University and is currently enrolled in the Masters in Humanities Program at Dominican University of California.

Eric Shattuck is a freelance writer living in Charleston, South Carolina. He studied at South Carolina State University, where he earned a Bachelor of Arts in English and served as an editor for the Inkwell Student Literary Journal. His work has been published or is forthcoming in *Gone Lawn, Freeze Frame Fiction, 99 Pine Street, Yellow Chair Review, Nottingham Review,* and *The Drabblecast.*

Patricia Shultheis has been a lecturer in the Odyssey Program of Johns Hopkins University. Her short story collection, *St. Bart's Way,* is the 2015 winner in fiction from the Washington Writers Publishing House, and in 2007 her pictorial local history, *Baltimore's Lexington Market,* was published by Arcadia Publishing. Other honors include awards from The Fitzgerald Writers' Conference, Memoirs Ink, and the American League of American Pen Women, Nob Hill Branch and Winning Writers. Patricia has been a fellow at the Virginia Center for the Creative Arts, and has served on the editorial boards of *The Baltimore Review* and *Narrative.* She is a member of The Author's Guild, as well as The National Book Critics Circle, and holds degrees from Albertus Magnus College and Johns Hopkins University.

Emmaline Silverman is a librarian and poet living in the suburbs of Washington, DC. Her poems have appeared in *Rust+Moth, Clementine (Unbound), Pankhearst Fresh,* and elsewhere in print and online.

Danny Earl Simmons is an Oregonian and a proud graduate of Corvallis High School. He is a friend of the Linn-Benton Community College Poetry Club and currently serves on its Poetry Advisory Committee. His poems have appeared in a variety of journals, such as *The Pedestal Magazine, Little Patuxent Review, Ithaca Lit, San Pedro River Review,* and *Off the Coast,* where he now assists as a member of the editorial staff.

Judith Skillman's new book is *Kafka's Shadow,* Deerbrook Editions. Her poems have appeared in *Cimarron Review, Shenandoah, Tampa Review, FIELD, Poetry,* and elsewhere. Awards include an Eric Mathieu King Fund grant from the Academy of American Poets. She is the author of a 'how to': *Broken Lines—The Art & Craft of Poetry.* Skillman has done collaborative translations from French, Portuguese, and Macedonian. Visit www.judithskillman.com.

William R. Soldan received his BA in English Literature from Youngstown State University, where he was formerly the head fiction editor of the student-run online literary magazine *Jenny.* He currently studies fiction and poetry in the Northeast Ohio MFA program and teaches English Composition at YSU. His work has appeared or is forthcoming in a number of publications, such as *New World Writing, The Vignette Review, Jellyfish Review, Elm Leaves Journal, Thuglit,* and others. He lives in Youngstown, Ohio, with his wife and son.

Susan Sonde's poems have appeared in *The North American Review, Barrow Street, Cimarron Review, Epoch, Narrative Magazine* (poem of the week), *The New Mexico Humanities Review,* and many others. Her collection, *In the Longboats with Others,* won The Capricorn Book Award and was published by New Rivers Press. Her chapbook, *Drumming on Water,* was recently published by Finishing Line Press.

Peter J. Stavros is a writer in Louisville, Kentucky. His work has appeared in *The Boston Globe Magazine, Fiction Southeast, Juked* and *Literary Orphans,* among others. More can be found at peterjstavros.wordpress.com.

Christina Sun is a senior at the University of Massachusetts Amherst and has work featured in *Word Riot, The Adroit Journal, Gravel,* and elsewhere. She writes and spams at christinaashleysun.wordpress.com.

Daniel J. Sundahl is Emeritus Professor in English and American Studies of Hillsdale College where he taught for more than 32 years. He and his wife Ellen have relocated from Michigan to South Carolina.

Aden Thomas grew up in central Wyoming. His poems have appeared in *Kentucky Review, The Inflectionist Review, Up the Staircase Quarterly,* and *Dressing Room Poetry Journal.* He lives in Laramie, Wyoming. More of his work can be found at adenthomas.com.

Alex Thomas, a recent graduate of Salisbury University in Maryland, currently resides in Washington, DC. His poetry appears in *Red Paint Hill, Slipstream* and elsewhere.

Travis Truax earned his bachelor's degree in English from Southeastern Oklahoma State University in 2010. His work has appeared or is forthcoming in *Flyover Country, Marathon Literary Review, Flagler Review,* and *The Eastern Iowa Review.* After college he spent several years working in various national parks in the West. He currently lives in Bozeman, Montana.

Eric Twardzik is a fiction writer and journalist living in Boston. His fiction has appeared in *The Emerson Review, Glass Mountain* and Ivy-Style.com. His nonfiction has been featured in *The Boston Phoenix, Dig Boston* and Vice.com. He is a graduate of the creative writing program at Emerson College.

Samuel Vargo writes journalism for a number of liberal, online, national magazines that headline daily. He also writes for a few comedy and satire mags with an international readership that also headline daily. He has written poetry and short stories for print and online literary magazines, university journals and a few commercial magazines and has worked most of his adult life as a newspaper reporter. He has a BA in Political Science and an MA in English (both from Youngstown State University). Vargo was the fiction editor of Pig Iron Press, Youngstown, Ohio, for 12 years. He was a curator and editor for a string of eight commercial online magazines for almost a year, but gave this up to work on his own writing pursuits. A book-length collection of Vargo's short stories, titled *Electric Onion Head and the Rotating Cyclops of the Month,* was published by Literary Road and had a web presence for five years.

Donna Vitucci is Development Director of Covington Ladies Home, the only freestanding personal care home exclusively for older women in Northern Kentucky. She is a life-long writer, and was a finalist for the Bellwether Prize in 2010. Her short fiction has appeared in dozens of print and online journals and anthologies. Her first novel, *At Bobby Trivette's Grave,,* takes place in Paris, KY, ninety miles south of Donna's home in Covington's Historic Licking Riverside District. *Salt of Patriots,* her novel concerning families & uranium processing in 1950s Fernald, OH, arrives April 2017 from Rebel ePublishers.

Lillo Way's full-length manuscript, *Wingbone,* was a finalist for the 2015 Barry Spacks Poetry Prize, and her chapbook manuscript, *The Life We've Slept Here,* was a finalist in the 2015 Grayson Books Chapbook Competition. Her poems have appeared in *Poet Lore, Tampa Review, Madison Review, The Sow's Ear Poetry Review, Poetry East, Common Ground Review, Third Wednesday, Yemassee, Santa Fe Literary Review, WomenArts Quarterly, Marathon Literary Review* and *SLAB,* among many others. Five of her poems have been anthologized in the "Good Works" series of FutureCycle Press.

Anna Lowe Weber currently lives in Huntsville, Alabama, where she teaches creative writing at the University of Alabama in Huntsville. Her work has appeared or is forthcoming in *Rattle, Salamander, Ninth Letter,* and the *Florida Review,* among other journals.

Ellie White holds a BA in English from The Ohio State University and an MFA from Old Dominion University. She writes poetry and nonfiction and is the creator of the online comic strip "Uterus & Ellie." Her work has appeared in *Antiphon Poetry Magazine, Harpur Palate, Tincture,* and several other journals. Ellie's chapbook, *Requiem for a Doll,* was released by ELJ Publications in June 2015. She is a nonfiction editor at *Four Ties Literary Review,* and the Social Media Editor for *Muzzle Magazine.* She currently lives near some big rocks and trees outside Charlottesville, Virginia.

Now retired from her career as a college administrator and communications professor, **Jill White** has become an award-winning jewelry artist and poet. Her poetry has appeared in numerous literary journals, including *U.S. 1 Worksheets, The Poetry Quarterly, Olentangy Review, Cumberland River Review, Stoneboat Journal, Rust+Moth, Yellow Chair Review,* and *Dead Mule School of Southern Literature.* If not at the writing desk or jewelry bench, she can be found with her nose in a book and a cat at her feet.

John Sibley Williams is the editor of two Northwest poetry anthologies and the author of nine collections, including *Controlled Hallucinations* (FutureCycle Press, 2013) and *Disinheritance* (Apprentice House, 2016). A five-time Pushcart nominee and winner of the Philip Booth Award, American Literary Review Poetry Contest, Nancy D. Hargrove Editors' Prize, and Vallum Award for Poetry, John serves as editor of *The Inflectionist Review* and works as a literary agent. Previous publishing credits: *The Midwest Quarterly, december, Third Coast, Baltimore Review, Nimrod International Journal, Hotel Amerika, Rio Grande Review, Inkwell, Cider Press Review, Bryant Literary Review, RHINO,* and various anthologies. He lives in Portland, Oregon.

Paul Willis is a professor of English at Westmont College and a former poet laureate of Santa Barbara, California. He recently served as an artist-in-residence in North Cascades National Park. His latest collection is *Getting to Gardisky Lake* (Stephen F. Austin State University Press, 2016). Website: pauljwillis.com.

Martin Willitts Jr. won the 2014 Dylan Thomas International Poetry Contest; the *Rattle* Ekphrastic Challenge, Editor's Choice (June 2015); and the *Rattle* Ekphrastic Challenge, Artist's Choice (November 2016). He has more than 20 chapbooks to his credit, including the *Turtle Island* Editor's Choice Award-winning *The Wire Fence Holding Back the World* (Flowstone Press, 2016), and ten full-length collections, including National Ecological Award Winner *Searching for What You Cannot See* (Hiraeth Press, 2013), *How to Be Silent* (FutureCycle Press, 2016), and *Dylan Thomas and the Writing Shed* (FutureCycle Press, 2017).

Cody Wilson teaches high school English in Peoria, Arizona. He is an MFA candidate at Queens University of Charlotte and is a poetry reader for *Qu,* the program's literary magazine.

Annie Woodford is a teacher and poet living in Roanoke, Virginia. Her poetry has appeared or is forthcoming in *Appalachian Heritage, The Comstock Review, Word Riot, The Normal School, The Chattahoochee Review, Waccamaw, Bluestem,* and *Town Creek Poetry,* among others.

Chila Woychik is a late-emerging female writer of German birth and amorphous Cherokee heritage most at home hiking in the woods or regarding coyote calls at night. She has work published or forthcoming in *Silk Road, Emrys, Blueline,* and others. She is also managing editor at *Eastern Iowa Review.*

About FutureCycle Press

FutureCycle Press is dedicated to publishing lasting English-language poetry books, chapbooks, and anthologies in both print-on-demand and Kindle formats. Founded in 2007 by long-time independent editor/publishers and partners Diane Kistner and Robert S. King, the press incorporated as a nonprofit in 2012. A number of our editors are distinguished poets and writers in their own right, and we have been actively involved in the small press movement going back to the early seventies.

The FutureCycle Poetry Book Prize and honorarium is awarded annually for the best full-length volume of poetry we publish in a calendar year. Introduced in 2013, our Good Works projects are anthologies devoted to issues of universal significance, with all proceeds donated to a related worthy cause. Our Selected Poems series highlights contemporary poets with a substantial body of work to their credit; with this series we strive to resurrect work that has had limited distribution and is now out of print.

We are dedicated to giving all of the authors we publish the care their work deserves, making our catalog of titles the most diverse and distinguished it can be, and paying forward any earnings to fund more great books.

We've learned a few things about independent publishing over the years. We've also evolved a unique, resilient publishing model that allows us to focus mainly on vetting and preserving for posterity the most books of exceptional quality without becoming overwhelmed with bookkeeping and mailing, fundraising activities, or taxing editorial and production "bubbles." To find out more about what we are doing, come see us at futurecycle.org.